THE EXTRAORDINARY WOMEN IN THE BIBLE

A special study to enable you to rediscover the unique nature of the Greatest Book of ALL TIME.

By Bible Scholar
Dr Gilbert Rethual BSc., MBBS, MD(USA)

GW00720747

ARTHUR H. STOCKWELL LTD.
Torrs Park   Ilfracombe   Devon
Established 1898
www.ahstockwell.co.uk

British Library Cataloguing-in-Publication Data.
A catalogue record for this book is available
from the British Library.

Arthur H. Stockwell Ltd. bears no responsibility
for the accuracy of events recorded in this book.

Acknowledgement

The author would like to thank the American Bible Society and GOOD NEWS BIBLE for the noble and charitable deed — producing the Bible for the masses to comprehend the language and message easily.

The quotations in this book are taken from the Today's English Version (TEV) unless otherwise stated. Much of the text, however, is written in the paraphrased style of the author with his understanding through more than half a century of Christian education. For this he publicly thanks all his Christian educators, and Almighty God for inspiring him in this project.

ISBN 0 7223 3676-4
Printed in Great Britain by
Arthur H. Stockwell Ltd.
Torrs Park   Ilfracombe
Devon

Dedication

To the memory of my mother Mary, my mother-in-law Rosari, the kind widows, and all the good women who helped me in my life.

Why did I dedicate this book to all the good widows? Because I know the true story of one good widow. She was widowed at the age of twenty-two. She had three children under four years of age, the youngest being nineteen days old.

The husband was gunned down in front of the wife and children. Their house was ransacked and their car and other valuables stolen.

Suddenly, they were thrown into a different gear. The date was January 20, 1943. It was a very difficult and tiring time because the whole world was at war. Chaos was everywhere. There were no shops or supplies available. Nobody wanted a young widow with three very young children. The future looked very bleak. Even relatives shunned them, considering them a burden — a liability. They moved on from house to house and town to town to finally settle down in a remote part of the world near the Malaysia-Thailand border.

The children grew up in foster homes without much love and affection from relatives and friends. Their only consolation was the love of the mother and the inspirational stories from the Bible.

One son of this widow managed to get into postgraduate doctoral studies in different continents and made his mother proud. He came a long way from the obscure town in Malaysia to settle down in the USA. He has written a number of books, performed in music concerts and kept his promise to his mother that he would write a book on the women of the Bible.

Yes, yours truly went around the world and after much research in the Holy Land, he has made this book a reality. Part of the funds from the sales of this book will go to help the widows and orphans.

God bless all the poor widows and all those who help them.

The word of God is not bound, it transcends cultures, geographical barriers and ethnic diversities. It speaks to the human soul, and meets several human needs. Unbiased please read on, prayerfully.

There is joy in the Bible: Discover this.
There is Love in the Bible: Discover this.
There is poetry and dance: Discover these.

Your neck is like a tower of ivory.
Your eyes are like the pools in the city of Hesbon. . . .
Your nose is as lovely as the tower of Lebanon. . . .
Your head is held high like Mount Carmel.
Your braided hair shines like the finest satin;
Its beauty could hold a king captive.
How pretty you are, how beautiful. . . .

(The Song of Solomon 7:4-6)

About the Author

Dr Gilbert Rethual is a Bible scholar who believes that one should have a scientific approach towards the Bible. He has travelled extensively throughout the Bible Lands, in the Middle East, Asia Minor, the Aegean Sea, following the missionary journeys of St Paul and then on to the Roman Peninsula. In January 2002 he started the CBS* in Los Angeles.

He has more than twenty years of formal instruction in Christian institutions and this has spurred him to know more. He has given lectures after participating in Christian archeological projects in Anatolia.

He is an excellent speaker on a variety of topics, including Nutrition and Alternative Medicine. He also has additional qualifications in these areas of healing, but he strongly believes that the Bible itself is a healing agent, an antidote to the many diseases of the mind and psychosomatic illnesses. Jesus Christ, according to him, is the greatest stress-buster. He came here specifically to teach us methods of coping with stress. He is the Life, the Light, the Leaven to lift your spirits and the Love you must know.

*Christian Bible Service — a Center for Service and Research in the Bible.

Contents

Motivation

Why a book on Women of the Bible?

Because women are motivators. (Remember: The hand that rocks the cradle rules the world.)

What is Motivation?

So much has been written about this word that it confuses those who seek to know it. Here is a simple explanation and an example: The key word is MOVE. Motivation comes from the Latin word *Movere*, meaning movement. Remember, only live things and people move. Since you are alive and reading this you must know it concerns you. To be alive totally and be moving in the right direction you also need to read this book. This book is special as it concerns the segment of mankind responsible for making lots of movement. Yes, I'm referring to the women. Now, coming back to motivation, you must realize that movement can be slow or moderate or fast. There are times when you have to slow down your movements. When you are at prayer, or during meditation, your communication channels are dealing with a different sphere. You can close your eyes, shut your mouth or even silence your ears, and in the process lower your heart rate and respiratory rate. The movement is still there, reaching out to God. You make your moves to contact God and let God move to help you.

At times you want fast action and this requires fast movements. The whole problem of restless youth on the rampage destroying valuable property is because of the inability to get quick action on many matters. The pace of activity in the world has increased and everything has an accent of speed.

Movement must be in the right direction and at a comfortable speed. You have probably heard of mothers who were motivators of great personalities in history. Some motivators are called

11

counsellors, psychologists, shrinks, psychotherapists, psychiatrists, psychoanalysts and even stressologists. Some priests and religious leaders have also joined the ranks of motivators. But the best motivator of all is the Bible.

Herein is the inspired Word of God to help us move in our journey on the long and difficult way to the final goal — Heaven. We are all travellers and are daily moving amidst the temptations and various stressors that beam on us or touch us. This book is a motivational book to help you look at life in a positive manner and accept things as they come. Do not fret and frown if things don't go the way you want them to go, but accept them as they occur.

Even in the Bible there are interesting stories where things did not turn out right to a lot of good people. This brings you face-to-face with the question you always asked yourself: why do bad things happen to good people? Or, to put it in another way, you may have seen the happy-go-lucky guy driving a Ferrari and wondered: how come good things happen to some not-so-good people?

You must motivate yourself to do the right things and not bother with how God blesses the other person. In due time everything will turn out right. All you've got to do is to keep moving closer to God, by doing good deeds. Learn from stories of how the good women played their part and helped the human race. Think also of those who helped you. Now move on to spread the good news of the Lord. The Bible is your best example for help in times of distress.

Thoughts to help you to move rightly and cope with fear.

1 — Fear not to reach out to God daily.

2 — Fear not to reach out to some who are in trouble.

3 — Put your faith in the Lord and do the thing you fear most. This way you will kill fear.

4 — Fear is a person's greatest enemy and it is responsible for your bad moves, your bad moods and even your aggressive nature.

5 — Fear not to make your move to change your aggressive and unkind attitude.

6 — Fear causes stagnation, hesitation and a withdrawal move. It is thus negative.

7 — Suggestive amnesia that strikes during or just before examinations is only due to fear. Overcome this by declaring positive affirmations boldly: "I have a good memory. I am brilliant. I know it too well."

8 — Make your moves to banish abnormal fear. After all it is only a natural feeling if it is in defence of your body.

9 — Tell your fears to move off. Learn to laugh at your fears. That is the best antidote: "Why should I fear?"

10 — The great law of substitution is another antidote to fear. The solution is in your heart. If you are afraid of failure, think or visualize success. If you are afraid of illness or ill-will, think of God's good protection. If you fear being trapped, desire freedom. Move your mental picture slides to good and happy scenes. The rest is up to Divine Assistance.

11 — What is the little child's greatest fear? It is the fear of falling down. This is why the child-toddler clings to the mother for support.

12 — In the aftermath of the September 11 attacks a great sense of fear gripped the USA and this had its repercussions worldwide: fear of opening letters (anthrax); fear of air travel; fear of a bearded person wearing a keffiyeh headdress.

How do mothers overcome fear? They sing a lullaby. How can you overcome it as an adult? Read the inspirational stories from the Bible.

The Bible

The Bible is undoubtedly the most widely read book in the world. It has been translated into all the major languages. What makes it so interesting is the people in it; people like you and me and the person next door.

In this book many characters come alive, but on purpose I have selected only the women. This is to answer a long-time need to get them some more prominence. Luke's Gospel is full of women and events connected with them; more so than in any other Gospel. He was a physician and I share the same interests. I have been involved in the health and care of women and had a maternity home to look after their special needs. When I became a counsellor and a psychotherapist I found women had extra special needs.

After all, biologically and emotionally there are major differences. They are a later creation and so are better equipped for special roles. These days I feel they handle stress far better than men. They don't become serial killers; they don't do highway shootings, or run amok with knives or guns; they do not do 'Hara-Kiri'; they don't do school shootings and bombings; they are not the ones responsible for the 11th September hijack disasters in the USA and other acts of terrorism. There are *rara avis* and *femme fatale* but, generally, most women are the kinder of the species. Very often they are the victims. There are some who have effected major changes in society and are currently the power behind very successful men.

The Extraordinary Women in the Bible should give you an insight to a variety of women mentioned in the Bible. Discover them and you will discover some of their kind — in existence even now —

who can touch your life and influence it.

God made man in His image and this was different from the process of evolution as advanced by the theories of Darwin. When man was created it was for a special purpose. It was for God to have a meaningful dialogue and relationship with the human. No animal could do that, nor the hypothetical "missing link".

God created the human with the human mind. It is with this mind that the human was supposeu to meditate, pray and act with Faith, Hope and Charity.

The woman was a later special creation and, in a way, an improved version of the human, endowed with sentiments and concerns.

You are a special creation. Read this book and discover the women of the Bible. May this venture and the reflections make you use your mind to glorify the Creator with your actions.

Roman soldiers carrying away the seven-branched menorah from the Temple of Jerusalem. Trajan's Arch in Rome.

The Bible Books

The Bible is composed of a "library" of sixty-six Books. The New Testament has twenty-seven Books.

According to the Old Testament there are thirty-nine Books. The first Book is Genesis (meaning origin) and Chapters 1-11 deal with Creation.
Chapters 12-50 deal with the history of the Israelites till their slavery in Egypt. Exodus is the second Book. The last Book is that of the Prophet Malachi.

The Synoptic Gospels are Matthew, Mark and Luke. The non-Synoptic Gospel is John.
Mark's Gospel is the first written Bible Book. He is believed to have written with instructions from Peter. John Mark is buried in the Basilica in Venice.
The Gospel of Matthew is believed to be the second Bible book that was written. Matthew, a tax collector by profession and a well-educated man, may have made references from Mark and the Q text. He wrote between AD 40 and AD 50.
Luke was a Greek and considered a gentile. He was the physician to the Apostles. He is the author of the Gospel that bears his name and the Book, the Acts of the Apostles. He made references to Mark and the Q text. His Gospel has the most references to women and also to diseases.
John's Gospel is the last Gospel written. He was related to Jesus (first cousin). He also wrote the Book of Revelation. The books were written from the period AD 60-100.
The Letters of St Paul were written by Paul, a Jew convert. He was highly educated. The letters are historical and relate to events of the early Church. He greatly influenced Christian thinking.

The Old Testament Books are:

Genesis*	2 Chronicles	Daniel
Exodus*	Ezra	Hosea
Leviticus*	Nehemiah	Joel
Numbers*	Esther	Amos
Deuteronomy*	Job	Obadiah
Joshua	Psalms	Jonah
Judges	Proverbs	Micah
Ruth	Ecclesiastes	Nahum
1 Samuel	Song of Songs	Habakkuk
2 Samuel	Isaiah	Zephaniah
1 Kings	Jeremiah	Haggai
2 Kings	Lamentations	Zechariah
1 Chronicles	Ezekiel	Malachi

*Pentateuch (Torah Books)

The New Testament Books and Letters are:

Matthew*	Ephesians	Hebrews
Mark*	Philippians	James
Luke*	Colossians	1 Peter
John*	1 Thessalonians	2 Peter
Acts	2 Thessalonians	1 John
Romans	1 Timothy	2 John
1 Corinthians	2 Timothy	3 John
2 Corinthians	Titus	Jude
Galatians	Philemon	Revelation

*Evangelists

The languages of the Bible

The Old Testament was written mostly in Hebrew and the rest in Aramaic, a Syrian dialect. The New Testament was entirely written in Greek, as this was the spoken and written language in the first and second centuries.

Should there be four Gospels?

Yes, only four Gospels.

Why? Because these were divinely inspired. God had a purpose to have four different representatives. Read between the lines and you will realize this.

There are four basic needs of the people to be met, with regard to salvation:

1 — A leader, a king — to deliver them from the woes. Matthew presented Jesus as a king — the legal heir — to please the Jews.

2 — A spiritual and intellectual person — unlike any other. God made man. John presented Jesus as God. He gave details in philosophical, metaphorical and direct terms to justify Jesus as God. He wrote for the scholars.

3 — The working man is part of a hierarchy. The suffering worker is a servant in such a system. Mark presented Jesus as one who worked miracles and who was interested in workers — the common sufferers. Jesus is the suffering Messiah, who understands the workers — in a set-up under foreign domination.

4 — The Greek world of the Gentiles needed a Messiah. There was much confusion with regard to religion — and too many gods. Luke, the physician, expressed his "report" in a scholarly manner to the Greeks. His Gospel has many references to women. Christ is the true Redeemer (23:8; 24:21).

The categories and the seven divisions of the Bible:

History — The story of the earliest peoples of the Bible, considered the "Chosen People" with their entry into the Promised Land (Canaan), also their exiles and return. The Gospels and the Acts of the Apostles contain historical accounts.

Law — The Five Scrolls (Pentateuch).

The Wisdom and Poetry — There are sayings of wisdom.

Prophecy — The role of the Prophets who advise and guide.

The Letters — Paul's Letters and that of the other Apostles on advice and activities.

Revelation — Letters to the Seven Churches in Asia Minor.

The Apocrypha — The collection of Books on the Old Testament and about Jesus. Following the Reformation, the Roman Catholic Church decided at the Council of Trent (1546) to include some Apocryphal Books that were written between the time of Malachi and the four Gospels.

These are not accepted by the Jews and some Christian Churches. This was because it was felt these books did not meet the standard (Canon). The word canon means "rule" or "authoritative and divine". The Old Testament with thirty-nine Books was automatically Canonical and the Council of Carthage declared the twenty-seven Books of the New Testament Canonical in AD 397.

Are all Christian Bibles the same?

The correct answer is no. There are notable differences between the Catholic and Protestant (especially the Lutheran and Episcopalian) Bibles. This is in the area of the Old Testament Books.

The Council of Trent in AD 1546 met for eight years and completed the "canonizing" of the Bible. The Books not included by the Protestants are: 1 Maccabees, 2 Maccabees, Tolbit, Judith, Sirach, Wisdom and Baruch; there are also some additions to the Books of Daniel and Esther.

Catholics refer to these as deutero-canonical (second listed). Some Protestants include these under Apocrypha (hidden or secret, and also implying not inspired).

The Lutherans and Episcopalians also have their uniqueness with the inclusion of: 1 Esdras, 2 Esdras and the Prayer of Manasseh. These are part of their Apocrypha.

The Septuagint — This term means seventy for the number of Jewish scholars who translated the Old Testament into Greek.

The Vulgate — This term means common. The Latin Vulgate Version was done by St Jerome in the 4th Century.

The Douay-Rheims Version — From the French towns of the above name. English Catholic scholars translated the Latin Vulgate into English in the 16th century.

Authorized Version — This is the English version for the Protestant Church. In the United States this was promoted as the King James Version from 1611 among the Protestant Churches. A version of this is the Revised Standard Version which was first published in 1952.

Bible quotations: (from St Paul)

I send greeting to Priscilla and Aquila, my fellow-workers in the service of Christ Jesus; they risked their lives for me. I am grateful to them — not only I, but all the Gentile Churches as well *(Romans 16:3-4)*.

But when the right times finally came, God sent forth his own Son. He cane as the Son of a human mother. . . . *(Galatians 4:4)*.

My greetings to Tryphaena and Tryphosa, who work in the Lord's service and to my dear friend Persis, who has done so much work for the Lord. I send greetings to Rufus. . . . and to his mother, who has always treated me like a son *(Romans 16:12-13)*.

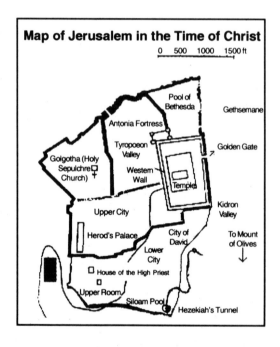

Map of Jerusalem in the Time of Christ

0   500   1000   1500 ft

Pool of Bethesda

Gethsemane

Antonia Fortress

Tyropoeon Valley

Golden Gate

Golgotha (Holy Sepulchre Church)

Western Wall

Temple

Upper City

Kidron Valley

Herod's Palace

City of David

To Mount of Olives

Lower City

House of the High Priest

Upper Room

Siloam Pool

Hezekiah's Tunnel

The Temple of Solomon

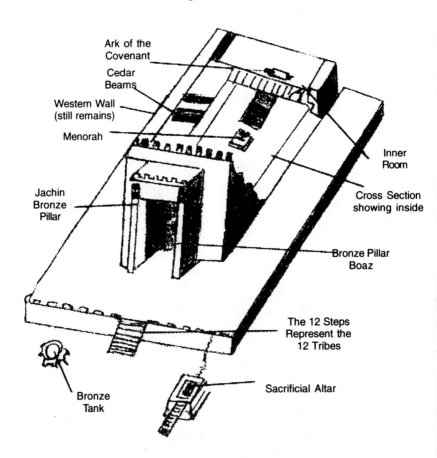

Ark of the Covenant

Cedar Beams

Western Wall (still remains)

Menorah

Jachin Bronze Pillar

Inner Room

Cross Section showing inside

Bronze Pillar Boaz

The 12 Steps Represent the 12 Tribes

Bronze Tank

Sacrificial Altar

The Temple of Solomon was built 458 years after the Israelites left Egypt, in the fourth year of King Solomon's reign.

The work commenced in the second month (Ziv) and it took seven years to complete. David purchased the land for the Temple construction.

It was broken down a few times. Herod the Great rebuilt it very magnificently between 4 BC and 2 BC.

23

Brief chronology of the Bible

Period of Darkness
Prehistory — CREATION — 6 "DAYS"
      — Adam
      — Eve   } Period of humans in Paradise
      — Cain, Abel & Seth
      — Noah and the Flood
      — The Tower of Babel

BC   Shem Terah-Abraham
2000   Lot, Abraham's nephew
      Abraham & Sarah
      Ishmael
      Isaac
      Jacob, son of Isaac
      Jacob's twelve sons & one daughter, Dinah
      Joseph in Egypt
      Jacob's descendants enslaved in Egypt (1700 BC - c.1290 BC)
      Moses the deliverer
      Forty years of wandering in the Sinai Desert
      Joshua leads the Jews to Promised Land
      Period of Judges in Canaan

BC   Samuel
1000   First King Saul c.1030 - c.1010
      Second King David — United Kingdom c.1010 - c.970
      Third King Solomon c.970 - 931
      Two divided kingdoms

South Kingdom — Judah		*North Kingdom — Israel*	
Rehoboam	931 - 913	Jeroboam	931 - 910
Abijah	913 - 911	Nadab	910 - 909
Asa	911 - 870	Baasha	909 - 886
Jehoshaphat	870 - 848	Elah	886 - 885
Jehoram	848 - 841	Zimri	885 (7 days)
Ahaziah	- 841	Omri	885 - 874
Queen Athaliah	841 - 835	Ahab	874 - 853
Joash	835 - 796	Ahaziah	853 - 852
Amaziah	796 - 781	Joram	852 - 841
Uzziah	781 - 740	Jehu	841 - 814
Jotham	740 - 736	Johoahaz	814 - 798
Ahaz	736 - 716	Jehoash	798 - 783
Hezekiah	716 - 687	Jeroboam II	783 - 743
Manasseh	687 - 642	Zechariah	743 (6 mths)
Amon	642 - 640	Shallum	743 (1 mth)
Josiah	640 - 609	Menahem	743 - 738
Joahaz	609 (3 mths)	Pekahiah	738 - 737
Jehoiakim	609 - 598	Pekah	737 - 732
Jehoiachin	598 (3mths)	Hoshea	732 - 723
Zedekiah	598 - 587	Fall of Samaria	- 722

Exile into Babylonia	605 onwards
Jerusalem sacked (Fall of Jerusalem)	July 587
Persian Rule	539
Jews return to Jerusalem	538
New Temple rebuilt	520
Greek rule in Palestine (Alexander the Great)	333
Rule by Alexander's generals (the Ptolemies)	323 - 198
Palestine ruled by Seleucids (descendants of Alexander's generals)	198 - 166
Judas Maccabeus Revolt The Maccabeus family (Hasmoneans)	} 166 - 163
Roman rule begins with Roman general Pompey — Puppet kings appointed by Rome	} 63 BC
The infamous Herod the Great	37 BC - 4 BC
Pax Romana (Peace of Rome) declared — Census time	63 BC - 4 BC
Birth of John the Baptist	2 BC

Birth of Jesus	**Anno Domini**
John the Baptist's ministry	c. AD 25
Public Ministry of Jesus	3 years period
Death & Resurrection of Jesus	c. AD 30
Conversion of Paul (Saul of Tarsus)	AD 38
Mention of word Christian in Antioch	AD 40
Ministry of Paul	c. AD 41 - c. AD 65
Fall of Jerusalem to Titus	AD 70

The Holy Land

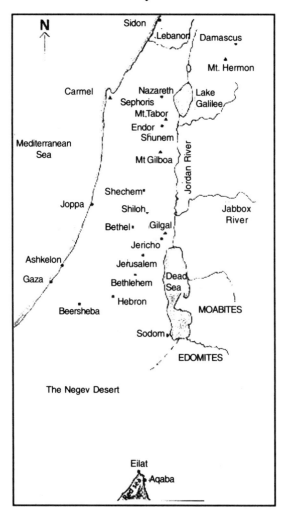

FACTS

Present-day ISRAEL covers a total land area of 25.975 sq. km. It is part of the Asian continent. Physical geography is dominated by the Rift Valley, which is the longest valley in the world. The Jordan River, Lake Coliloe and the Dead Sea, Arave Valley and Hula Valley are part of it. The Dead Sea is the lowest spot on the Earth at 400 metres below sea level. There are two seasons, winter and summer. There is snow on Mount Hermon and extreme heat — perhaps the hottest on Earth — at the Dead Sea shores.

Introduction

This book is intended to educate the curious and the casual reader of the Bible to appreciate the presence of women in the Bible.

Women are needed to be in the forefront of all activities in this world, and you don't have to listen to those who advocate theories that we are in this sorry mess all because of women. Of course, you know about the Taliban and the rights of women.

A woman is a special creature, created by the Almighty to be a companion to man. Without her man cannot have a full life. It's like the fact that you need both hands to clap to make a good sound of appreciation. However, if you are celibate it is different.

In this book some of the women are named by the author. The rest are reproduced in their original names. But, no one is really sure that these were the real names for the women characters. At times a nameless one was given a name befitting her role or the character she portrayed. This is in line with the "Veronica Connection". You may not have heard of this phrase. The Christian name Veronica is a very popular name all over the world. It is supposed to be the name of the saintly lady who ran out of the crowd and took a white handkerchief and wiped the blood-stained face of Jesus as He was on His way to Calvary. Veronica's Veil exists and copies of this are in museums and churches. Who was this Veronica? Well, she must have been real. We have a strong Christian tradition to suggest she did what she did. But she is the nameless one. In fact, there is no mention in any Bible about her existence. The sixth station of the Cross (out of the fifteen stations) is dedicated to her.

Even in Jerusalem on the Via Dolorosa the sixth station is a prominent place — where Veronica did the bold action of kindness which was not without risk.

In the same spirit of Veronica (the name in fact means true image, icon) names are given to some nameless women like the Samaritan woman at the well. The incidents are real, the message and the moral is real, but the name of the woman could be something else. It is necessary for us to know the message. That is important.

We cannot imagine a world without these women — a Bible without these women. Impossible! They are the species that make the Bible stories come to life. God must have wanted it that way. God's ways are mysterious ways.

Make a Resolution:

Do some good deeds each day.

Write down in a diary or notebook the good deeds that you do each day. You will realize that you need to make adjustments in your lifestyle to include the daily goodness.

Be happy.

Be gentle.

Be kind.

Be less angry.

Read the Bible often.

ABELA (The Woman of Abel)
2 Samuel 20-26

This is the story of a very bold woman. She must have been a young lady in her late twenties or early thirties. Why the age bracket? Because she is supposed to have climbed on the city wall and stood on it. Not only that, she is supposed to have yelled out loud to make the people hear her words. I am not saying that some old women cannot do what she did, but it requires a lot of adrenaline and she must have had lots of it either to volunteer to climb up the wall or to yell her head off to get the attention of a lot of angry men.

Israel and Judah were going through a difficult time during that period. There was a revolution and counter-revolution. Even King David's house was in rebellion. His beloved son, Absalom, rebelled against his father. Ahithophel misled young Absalom. They planned to kill King David and take his throne. David got the message and escaped across the River Jordan. In the battle Absalom was defeated and killed.

Then there was another rebellion from Sheba (a young warrior from Gilgal), son of King Bikri. He blew the trumpet and called out, "Down with King David! We won't follow him! Men of Israel, let's go home!" So a great number of soldiers deserted David, and these were not from Judah. These were the Israelites from the earlier North Kingdom. Anyway, David went back to Jerusalem and "took the ten concubines he had left to take care of the palace, and put them under guard. He provided for their needs". But he had to put down the rebellion of Sheba. So he sent Joab (his trusted commander), Abishai (Joab's brother) and some loyal soldiers in pursuit of Sheba, who had taken refuge in the city of Abel Beth Maacah. The clan of Bikri were also there with him in that city.

Joab's men besieged this city. They built ramps of earth on the sides of the city wall and also dug under the walls to weaken the structures so that they would fall. All these activities terrified the city folk. They had to do something. Joab was a fearless warrior. He was the one who was bold enough to plunge three spears into Absalom's chest while he was dangling from the oak tree. (David had earlier forbidden anyone from killing Absalom.) Joab would not spare the city folk for harbouring Sheba and his men.

Nobody wanted to be a hero. It was a risky business during the siege. This young woman decided to do something about it, otherwise the city would be razed to the ground and the people killed. The Bible says, "There was a wise woman in the city" *(2 Samuel 20:16)*. She climbed up the city wall. She stood on the wall and shouted out loud in spite of all the cacophony that existed. "Listen! Listen! Tell Joab to come here; I want to speak with him." She was indeed a very bold woman. It reminds us of the story of the Maid of Orleans, Joan of Arc.

Joab heard that he was wanted by a woman standing high up on the wall so he went to speak to her. She wanted him to identify himself. "Are you Joab?" she shouted out to him.

"Yes, I am," he answered.

"Then listen to me, sir. Long ago they used to say, 'Go and get your answer in the city of Abel' — and that is just what they did. Ours is a great city, one of the most peaceful and loyal in Israel. Why are you trying to destroy it?" She must have been really proud of her city — a local girl who loved the cobbled streets, the alleys, the market, the schools, the old rustic houses. She questioned Joab as if she did not know the real intention of Joab. Then, using psychology, she used her trump card and said, "Do you want to ruin what belongs to the Lord?"

Joab was taken aback. "Never! I will never ruin or destroy your city!" He then explained his real intention and why he was there.

I am sure by now the whole city was aware of the presence of Sheba and his men and why they were there in Abel Beth. Then Joab put forth his proposal, "Hand over this one man [Sheba], and I will withdraw from the city."

Then Abela, acting as a spokesperson for the city, shouted back, "We will throw his head over the wall to you."

Joab was pleased with the answer. Sheba dead or alive made no difference to him. Abela went to her people with her plan and soon they agreed. Sheba was captured and beheaded and his head thrown over the wall to Joab. The warrior blew his trumpet as a signal to ask his men to retreat and go home. Joab returned to Jerusalem to report to King David that he won the war with no loss of men (either to Joab or the enemy). Only one life was lost and that was the life of Sheba.

Abela thus saved the city and eased a lot of tension by her spirited effort. She was one real heroine.

David must have been extremely amused that his great warrior, Joab, quelled a rebellion with the assistance of one courageous woman.

Think It Over:

Courage should be second nature in a Christian. From Faith in the Lord comes Courage.

The Apostles ran away with fear for their lives when Jesus was arrested in the Garden of Gethsemane.

Courage returned to them, and, fortified with this virtue by the Holy Spirit, they proclaimed the Good News of Redemption and of the Gospels. If you have fears you have no Faith.

Dr G. Reth

ABIGAIL (Father's Joy)
1 Samuel 25

The story of Abigail is that of perhaps a beautiful, wise and practical lady. Some women are wise but not practical. On the other side of the coin there are also practical women who are not wise. Abigail was not only beautiful, she was a rich lady. Now, as if these virtues were not enough, let's add another feather in her cap: she was one rich lady who knew how to act with humility. Not all rich women can act humbly.

She was wise and intelligent because she knew how to handle stress. She will go down in Biblical history as one great stress-buster. Anyway, the greatest stress-buster of all is our Lord Jesus Christ — who came down on His earthly mission to show us the true way to handle day-to-day stressors, the good and the bad.

Now, coming back to Abigail — she was a rich man's wife. No details are given about the father, but with that name there is the suggestion that she was the apple of her father's eye. She must have been a really lively creature with all the qualities a father could be proud of.

The setting of the story is the town of Maon and this was close to Carmel on the western side of Israel. Samuel was dead and he was buried in his home in Ramah. David was the next in line to be King of Israel, but because of his tiff with King Saul, he was a fugitive living out in the wilderness of Paran with about four hundred men.

Nabal, Abigail's husband, was not a practical man. He is described as a very rich, but mean and bad-tempered man. This looks like the story of the beauty and the beast.

He was one who could not handle stress. (You may have all the money, and own the town and the land, but not having a good mind will undo everything.) He had 3,000 sheep and 1,000 goats.

Nabal (the name in Hebrew means fool) decided to hold a great feast for his sheep-shearers and friends. David and his armed men heard about this and wanted some food. They were hungry. In fact

David and his men were in the vicinity of Maon and Carmel and could have stolen some sheep or goats whilst they were grazing. They did no such thing. Also, they watched over the flock to see that no harm came to these animals or to the shepherds.

David sent ten young men with orders to go to Carmel, find Nabal and give him his greetings. He instructed them to say to Nabal: "David sends you greetings, my friend, with his best wishes for you, your family, and all that is yours. He heard that you were shearing your sheep, and he wants you to know that your shepherds have been with us and we did not harm them. Nothing that belonged to them was stolen all the time they were at Carmel. Just ask them, and they will tell you. We have come on a feast day, and David asks you to receive us kindly. Please give what you can to us your servants and to your dear friend David."

David's men delivered this message to Nabal in David's name. Then they waited there for a favourable answer. Nabal finally answered, "David ? Who is he? I've never heard of him! The country is full of runaway slaves nowadays! I'm not going to take my bread and water, and the animals I have slaughtered for my shearers, and give them to men who come from I don't know where!"

David's men went back to him and narrated what Nabal had said in such insulting terms. "Buckle on your swords!" he ordered, and they all did. David also buckled on his sword and left with about four hundred of his men, leaving behind two hundred to guard his supplies. David was a warrior and he was determined in his mind to kill Nabal's household and take the animals and his riches as his possessions.

Now comes the interesting part: one of the servants of Abigail overheard the encounter between David's men and Nabal. He narrated the whole incident to Abigail. "They were very good to us; they never bothered us and all the time we were in the fields nothing that belonged to us was stolen. They protected us day and night the whole time we were with them looking after our flocks. Please think this over and decide what to do. This could be disastrous for our master and all his family. He is so pigheaded that he won't listen to anybody!"

This was a stressful bit of news for Abigail. Yet she decided to handle it her way. She quickly gathered two hundred loaves of bread, two leather bags full of wine, five roasted sheep, two bushels of raisins, and two hundred cakes of dried figs and loaded them on donkeys. Then she asked the servants to go in the direction of the wilderness camp of David. "You go on ahead and I will follow you."

She rode fast on her donkey and soon she was in full sight of David and his armed men. She stopped abruptly, quickly dismounted and threw herself on the ground at David's feet. She said to him, "Please, sir, listen to me! Let me take the blame. Please, don't pay any attention to Nabal, that good-for-nothing! He is exactly what his name means — a fool! I wasn't there when your servants arrived, sir. It is the Lord who has kept you from taking revenge and killing your enemies. And now I swear to you by the living Lord that your enemies and all who want to harm you will be punished like Nabal. Please, sir accept this present I have brought you, and give it to your men. Please forgive me, sir, for any wrong I have done. The Lord will make you king, and your descendents also. . . . And when the Lord has blessed you, sir, please don't forget me."

David was overwhelmed by her humbleness. "Praise the Lord, the God of Israel, who sent you today to meet me! Thank God for your good sense and for what you have done today in keeping me from the crime of murder and from taking my own revenge. The Lord has kept me from harming you. But I swear by the living God of Israel that if you had not hurried to meet me, all of Nabal's men would have been dead by morning!" He then accepted the gifts. "Go back home and don't worry."

Abigail went back to Nabal and found him feasting. He was having a feast fit for a king. He was drunk and so she did not tell him the news right away — but did so next morning when he was sober. The news scared the daylights out of him — to realize that he was so close to death. He suffered a stroke and was completely paralysed. Some ten days later he died.

David decided to send a proposal of marriage to Abigail. His servants went to her at Carmel and said to her, "David sent us to take you to him to be his wife."

David knew she would be helpless as a widow and a wonderful, beautiful person left alone. She had all the virtues, he felt.

Abigail went to David's camp and bowed down to the ground and said, "I am his servant, ready to wash the feet of his servants. He later settled down in Hebron with her.

Abigail was involved in another incident in the Bible when she was kidnapped by the Amalekites, along with David's other wife Ahinoam and his children, while they were at Ziklag. The soldiers of David were also angry with David for losing their children.

David took along six hundred men and went to Besor Brook and sought the help of an Egyptian slave of an Amalekite who gave him details of where Abigail and the others were held. David attacked the Amalekites and rescued Abigail and the others and recovered all the accumulated loot of the raiders — the Amalekites.

Think It Over:

Opportunities come and go. Fools miss these. The wise make use of these. The villains capitalize on these for their selfish gains.

From the errors and omissions of the wise, one can gain wisdom for worthy actions.

Dr G. Reth

ADEL (The Adulterous Woman)

John 8:1-11

This lady could have been the victim of circumstances. Probably, she was not even an adulteress but just a fashionable girl. You probably have heard of the pretty girl next door — about whom there are stories that run in serials. Some girls are flirts and some look like flirts. Society loves gossip, stereotyping and even condemnation.

In this story, Jesus was in the Temple teaching early one morning. The teachers of the Law and the Pharisees brought in a woman who had been caught committing adultery, and they made her stand before them all. "Teacher," they said to Jesus, "this woman was caught in the very act of committing adultery. In our Law Moses commanded that such a woman must be stoned to death. Now, what do you say?"

They said this to trap Jesus, so that they could accuse Him. But He bent over and wrote on the ground with His finger. As they stood there asking Him questions, He straightened Himself up and said to them, "Whichever one of you has committed no sin may throw the first stone at her."

Then He bent over again and wrote on the ground. When they saw what He wrote and what He spoke they all left, one by one. Jesus was left alone with the woman still standing there. He straightened Himself up and said to her, "Where are your accusers? Is there no one left to condemn you?"

"No one, sir," she answered.

"Well, then," Jesus said, "I don't condemn you either. Go, but do not sin again."

There is a good point we can learn from this episode that has moral value. God knows our inner desires and our past sins and is a very forgiving God. To err is human — because our flesh is weak. God is the ultimate Judge who forgives sins.

Here we learn of God's mercy towards sinners. If we have offended someone, or God, it is natural to ask for forgiveness from the all-forgiving Father. Adel symbolizes many of us who sin or are caught in circumstances that suggest sin. Appeal to God. He can save you.

It is interesting to note in this incident that Adel did not even confess to Jesus that she was a sinful woman. Neither did she ask for forgiveness for her sins, yet the Master told her that her sins are forgiven and that she must avoid sin. God knows our conscience. He will forgive us as long as we speak to Him with a sincere mind and heart.

Remember:

GOD is ALL GOODNESS — GOD is ALL MERCIFUL
GOD is UNDERSTANDING — GOD is OMNIPOTENT
GOD is OMNIPRESENT — GOD is ALWAYS FORGIVING

We need to change our idea of God that was portrayed in the Old Testament. Jesus came with a specific purpose to teach us about God, who is a friend and a fellow-sufferer. He came to this earth and lived amongst us, but most of us did not recognize Him.

In this incident we learn of the love and concern Jesus has for us sinners. Instead of being God-fearing we should learn to be God-Loving. If we love Him, we will keep His commandments.

Who Is God?

God is the Supreme Being. There are three persons in God with three attributes. Hence the term, Holy Trinity.

The First Person is represented by the Father image. The second is the son — represented by Jesus Christ. The third is the Holy Spirit.

God has no beginning or end. Everything else is perishable.

ANNA (Hebrew: Hannah, Graceful)

Luke 2:36-37

Anna was a prophetess, the daughter of Phanuel of the tribe of Asher. She lived in the Temple of Jerusalem, worshipping the Lord, day and night, with fasting and penance. She was in the Temple when Jesus was brought in as an infant to be dedicated as the first-born male.

The other prophetesses in the Bible are Miriam, Deborah, and Huldah. These are holy women who have done God's good work and helped in the path of salvation. God gave them special blessings and graces — because of their virtues.

Anna was a widow. She was very old (eighty-four years) and had been married for only seven years when her husband died. When she saw the Baby Jesus she "gave thanks to God and spoke about the child to all who were waiting for God to set Jerusalem free".

The Temple of Jerusalem was a formidable structure. It became the focal point for Jews all over the world. Even in its broken state, with only one western wall remaining, it continues to attract worshippers.

The Temple was initiated by King David but built by his son Solomon (c.970-931 BC). With the fall of Jerusalem and the exile to Babylonia the Temple was destroyed in 587 BC. The second Temple was built with the Edict of Cyrus the Persian. In 538 BC the Jews returned. King Herod the Great improved on the Temple during 37 BC-4 BC.

The Roman General Titus, with help from his father Vespasian and brother Domitian, dispersed the Jews (the Diaspora). Titus destroyed the Temple in AD 70 and looted it.

ANNE (Hebrew: Hannah)

She was the wife of Joachim and grandmother of Jesus. She was the mother of Mary, the mother of Jesus. They were originally from Sephoris but settled down in Jerusalem in the vicinity of the Temple. Joachim was an official in the Temple. The house is still there, now restored — called St Anne's House. Historically, Sephoris, near Nazareth, was a great city. Archaeologists have discovered a synagogue and library.

She was an upright woman who, Christian tradition says, did her job to prepare the young Mary for her special duties — to be the mother of the Saviour.

There are many churches in the world dedicated to her. One of the most famous in the USA is in California, sixty miles south of Los Angeles and named Santa Ana. The whole area is named after her. In Asia there is the pilgrimage centre of St Anne in Bukit Mertajam, Penang, Malaysia — where thousands gather for the annual feast on 26th July.

Q. What is St Anne the patron of?
A. Generally, she is regarded as one who guides children along the right path. Good grandmothers do that.

Quotable Quotes:

Most of the glitter that we see in life first appeared as items that lacked lustre. Take diamond and coal, for instance. — *Dr G. Reth*

It is better to light a candle than to curse the darkness. — *Anon*

ATHALIAH (Israel's King Ahab's daughter)
2 Kings 11:1-3

She was married to Jehoram, King of Judah. Jehoram, the Scripture says, passed away to no one's regret and was buried in the city of David, but not in the tombs of the kings *(2 Chronicles 21:20)*.

Her son Ahaziah was crowned King of Judah. He did many things evil in God's sight. But God allowed him a very short reign — he ruled for one year. He was killed by "God's men" who were determined to destroy the evil regime and the household of King Ahab.

The person who seized the throne and ruled with Evil as her second name was Queen Athaliah. She slaughtered everyone in the royal family to stamp out opposition. The one who escaped was her grandson — son of Ahaziah. Princess Jehosheba and her husband hid this infant and took him to the Temple, where he was raised.

Queen Athaliah ruled for six years and she offended God by sacrilegious acts. She even went to the reserved sacred sections of the Temple and removed the sacred vessels and objects for worship. She used these to promote pagan worship.

Her grandson, Prince Joash, was raised in God-fearing ways and tutored by his aunt (Princess Jehosheba) and uncle (Jehoiada, the priest). As long as his aunt was alive he was a good king. When she died he surrounded himself with bad advisors who led to his downfall.

Some women love power and will do anything to keep power in their hands. Athaliah was one such person.

BATHSHEBA (Hebrew: Daughter of an Oath)

2 Samuel 11:2

Ironically, she comes into the scene of prominence in the Bible in a bath scene. David, the King of Israel, happened to be walking on the roof of the palace one evening and he saw a woman bathing.

The woman was very beautiful. So David sent someone to find out about her. The man said she was Bathsheba, the daughter of Eliam and the wife of Uriah the Hittite. *(2 Samuel 11:2-3)*.

Many Bible scholars do believe that Bathsheba was not completely an innocent party to the crime that David committed. The first crime was that of adultery with her the same night and fathering an illegitimate child. Then he committed a more grievous sin and that was arranging for the murder of Uriah, her husband. In this way she became free and David married her. Her first son through David died in his infancy.

Bathsheba also features in the lineage of Our Lord Jesus Christ, as her son Solomon reigned as King after King David.

David was clearly the culprit as he planned the whole episode to get this woman as his wife. She probably had no way to escape from a man as powerful as David. David treated Uriah like a good friend, ate and drank with him and planned well his murder. He sent him to the battlefield to be in the front line. He sent all the instructions to his Commander Joab. When Bathsheba heard that her husband had been killed, she mourned for him. When the time for mourning was over, David had her brought to his palace and she became his wife. David had a son through her but this son died an as infant.

Bathsheba is surely to be described as a different character from Abigail. Abigail would have sensed the sin and the consequences and stopped David somehow from committing adultery. She could also sense David's intention of acquiring her. Bathsheba could have resisted him or avoided him. She became his favourite wife and the mother of Solomon — a favoured son — David's heir.

Only God knows if Bathsheba was guilty. The prophet Nathan is depicted in the Bible as pointing out vividly that it was David's crime;

he does not implicate Bathsheba.

She was the daughter of an oath. What the oath was we do not know. Maybe some promise or prophecy was fulfilled by her birth.

Think It Over:

Did Bathsheba bring up Solomon well in the ways of a God-fearing or God-loving individual? Maybe she did.

Sometimes people change for the better. Sometimes people change for the worse.

Solomon destroyed all his earlier goodness and piety with his bad ways towards the end of his reign.

BEULAH (Beautiful)

Luke 13:10-13

One Sabbath Jesus was teaching in a synagogue. A woman there had an evil spirit that had made her ill for eighteen years; she was bent over and could not straighten up at all. When Jesus saw her, He called out to her, "Woman, you are free from your illness!"

He placed His hands on her, and at once she straightened herself up and praised God" *(Luke 13:10-13).*

The Jewish authorities of the synagogue were upset because Jesus did His healing on the Sabbath.

"There are six days in which we should work; so come during those days and be healed, but not on the Sabbath!"

Jesus was angry when He heard the Pharisees scolding the poor woman. In this case the woman had not even called out to Jesus to heal her. It was the compassion of Our Lord when He saw Beulah, sickly and bent over with a severe degree of kyphosis (spinal column bent forwards). He went out to her and placed His healing hands on her. She cannot be blamed at all. And even if she did call out it would have been to ask for help. This is no crime. It is for this that Jesus came to make changes in some sections of the Mosaic Law.

"You hypocrites!" Jesus shouted. "Any one of you would untie his ox or his donkey from the stall and take it out to give it water on the Sabbath. Now here is this descendant of Abraham whom Satan has kept bound up for eighteen years; should she not be released on the Sabbath?"

What Jesus said was very meaningful. Those who heard felt the wisdom in Jesus' words. We were made for the Sabbath and not the Sabbath made us — fashioned to our whims and fancies. Jesus made poor Beulah well and a lot of people felt what He did was good for the suffering woman.

We also learn here that suffering and pain are not inflicted by God. The evil one rejoices to put believers to suffering. Evil is everywhere.

CLAUDIA

Matthew 27:19

She was the Roman lady who was the wife of Pontius Pilate, the man who signed the execution order for the crucifixion of Jesus Christ. He was referred to as the Procurator of Jerusalem. This is similar to the position of the governor of the area of Israel. It was the highest position held by a Roman official in Israel, and he was answerable to the Roman Emperor, Caesar Augustus.

The Emperor proclaimed Pax Romana (the Peace of Rome) and levied taxes to carry out many construction projects. There were to be no more wars. Pontius Pilate's wife was a very influential lady. Most governor's wives are. But only Matthew, the tax collector, mentions her involvement in the story of Jesus. The other three Evangelists — Mark, Luke and John — do not mention her or quote her.

She, in spite of her powerful position, had no power to stop the execution order — or even the scourging or the hasty unfair trial. She knew Jesus was innocent. She even declared it so.

While Pilate was sitting in the judgement hall, his wife sent him a message: "Have nothing to do with that innocent man, because in a dream last night I suffered much on account of him" *(Matthew 27:19)*.

She did put in an effort. At least she tried; but it was useless because Pilate had fears of the civil unrest that could be levelled at him. It is the Will of God that the story should end this way, and Jesus submitted to the Will — "Thy Will be done". This sentence is there in the prayer that Jesus composed. The poignancy is shown here that many, even the governor's wife, knew that this was an innocent man, yet her husband condemned Him. Jesus symbolizes the innocent person who is condemned. You probably know of some. You need to take a stand and not wash your hands of any guilt.

DAMARIS (Hebrew: Gentle)

Acts 17:21

She was a follower of Paul, the self-styled Apostle of Jesus Christ, in Athens.

Paul had a tough time in Athens — because there were many idols and there was even an altar pedestal with the inscription for worship to an unknown god. While waiting for Silas and Timothy in Athens, Paul went about solo preaching about Jesus. The city elders took him before the city council, the Areopagus, and said, "We would like to know what this new teaching is that you are talking about. Some of the things we hear you say sound strange to us, and we would like to know what they mean".

So Paul preached about Jesus but there was much scepticism — especially when he spoke about resurrection. There were those who made fun of him. "Some men joined him and believed, among whom was Dionysius, a member of the council; there was also a woman named Damaris".

Gentleness was her name and she certainly heard the gentle news and it took root in her. We need to welcome and nurture this virtue in us. Gentleness is what God expects in every one of us. Education is a process to make us more gentle women and men.

Show a gentle attitude towards everyone. The Lord is coming soon. (Paul in his message to the Philippians.)

Damaris recognized Paul's gentleness and became his Apostle in Athens. This is why she is mentioned prominently as his follower.

DEBORAH (Hebrew: Bee, Greek: Melissa)
Judges 4:4-5

Deborah was a prophetess and the wife of Lappidoth. She held a special court to have disputes settled. She was a respected judge in a very difficult time in Israel's history.

Bees are very special creatures and you probably have heard of the expression 'as busy as a bee'. Deborah was kept real busy because Israel was in chaos. She had a mother image, thanks to her wisdom, and people from all walks of life came to her court, held under a palm tree, between Ramah and Bethel in the hill country of Ephraim.

Israel was under a Canaanite King called Jabin. One day she sent for Barak, son of Abinoam from the city of Kedesh in Naphtali and said to him, "The Lord, the God of Israel, has given you this command: 'Take ten thousand men from the tribes of Naphtali and Zebulun and lead them to Mount Tabor. I will bring Sisera, the commander of Jabin's army, to fight against you at the River Kishon He will have his chariots and soldiers, but I will give you victory over him'".

Then Barak replied, "I will go if you [Deborah] go with me, but if you don't go with me, I won't go either".

She answered, "All right, I will go with you, but you won't get any credit for the victory, because the Lord will hand Sisera over to a woman [me]". So Deborah set off for Kedesh because he insisted that she come. Barak called the tribes — and they came to number 10,000.

Sisera came with 900 iron chariots and his specially trained soldiers to the Kishon river. Deborah saw the forces and ordered Barak, "Go! The Lord is leading you! Today he has given you victory over Sisera". Barak went down from Mount Tabor with his 10,000 men. All Sisera's men were killed. Sisera ran away to the tent of Jael, who was the wife of Heber the Kenite. Jael went out to meet him and said to him, "Come in, sir; come into my tent. Don't be afraid". So he went in, and she hid him behind a curtain. There she killed him.

That day Deborah sang a song of praise for the Lord with Barak. "Praise the Lord! the Israelites were determined to fight, the people gladly volunteered. . . . The most fortunate of women is Jael, the wife of Heber the Kenite. . . . May all your enemies die like that, O Lord, but may your friends shine like the rising sun!"

It is to be noted that Deborah came into the scene because the land was in chaos. The people of Israel sinned against the Lord so He sent the Canaanite, King Jabin, to rule over them for twenty years. In their suffering they cried out to God and repented — Deborah was the only one who could command respect and give advice.

After the victory over Jabin and Sisera, there was peace in the land for forty years.

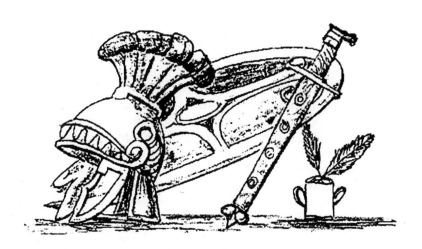

DELILAH (Hebrew: Beautiful Person)
Judges 15:16:4-22

Delilah was a lovely lady who lived in the Sorek Valley. Her beauty was well known to one and all. She was approached by five Philistine kings, who made a bargain with her: "Trick Samson into telling you why he is so strong and how we can overpower him, tie him up, and make him helpless. Each one of us will give you eleven hundred pieces of silver". Delilah accepted this proposal.

So Delilah went and charmed Samson and made him fall madly in love with her. Then she asked him admiringly, "Please tell me what makes you so strong. If someone wanted to tie you up and make you helpless, how could he do it?"

Samson answered, "If they tied me up with seven new bowstrings that are not dried out, I'll be as weak as anybody else".

The Philistine kings brought Delilah the required bowstrings and she tied him up. "Samson!" she shouted, "The Philistines are coming!" He snapped the strings easily. She knew she was fooled. Then she used more of her charms to entice him to tell her the secret. He fooled her again with lies. But she kept on pestering him day after day. He got so sick and tired of her bothering him about it he finally told her the truth. "My hair has never been cut," he said, "I have been dedicated to God as a Nazirite from the time I was born. If my hair were cut, I would lose my strength and be as weak as anybody else".

Delilah lulled Samson to sleep on her lap and cut off his seven locks of hair. Then she shouted, "Samson! The Philistines are coming!" He could not find the strength to untie himself. The Philistines captured him and made him blind and put him in prison to work grinding at the mill. After some time his hair grew back and he regained his strength. It was with this strength that the blind Samson could bring down the entire building wherein were Delilah, the five Philistine kings and a few thousand Philistines. All were trapped and killed by the destruction of the amphitheatre. Samson killed more people at his death than he killed during his life.

DINAH (Hebrew: Avenged)

Genesis 34,1-3

"One day Dinah, the daughter of Jacob and Leah, went to visit some of the Canaanite women".

Hamor the Hivite was a ruler and had a son named Shechem. Shechem saw Dinah and raped her. He told his father that he found her so attractive that he wanted to marry her. He expressed this desire to his father and asked him to negotiate with her parents.

Hamor went out to meet Jacob and ask him for his daughter in marriage. But Jacob's sons were furious that their sister was disgraced. Hamor told Jacob, "My son Shechem has fallen in love with your daughter; please let him marry her. Let us make an agreement that there will be intermarriage between our people and yours. Then you may stay here in our country with us; you may live anywhere you wish, trade freely, and own property".

Shechem also approached Dinah's brothers and tried to make friends with them. He told them, "Do me this favour, and I will give you whatever you want. Tell me what presents you want and set the payment for the bride as high as you wish; I will give you whatever you ask, if you only let me marry her" *(Genesis 34:11-12)*.

Dinah's brothers made a condition in a deceitful way to Shechem and Hamor. "We cannot let our sister marry a man who is not circumcised". In fact they wanted all the males to be circumcised. So they set out for the meeting place and spoke to the inhabitants to get their approval. The citizens agreed and they were circumcised.

Three days later, when the men were still sore from their circumcision, two of Dinah's brothers, Simeon and Levi, took their swords, went into the city without arousing suspicion, and killed all the men, including Hamor and his son Shechem" *(Genesis 34, 25-26)*.

They took Dinah, who was in Shechem's house, and left. Jacob's other sons then came in and looted the town. They took the flocks, the cattle, the donkeys, and everything in the city and in the fields. Everything of value was taken away — including the women and the children.

After this horrible incident Jacob left the area with his entourage to go and live in Bethel.

Jacob indeed was an extraordinary man. He is one who wrestled even with an angel. Many Jews believe that he dislocated his hip joint on account of this.

This aspect is considered in the kosher of meat involving the lamb's hip muscles.

Israel is the new name of Jacob, given by God after his wrestling with the angel.

Israel:

The land of Israel is a land of contrasts. The Dead Sea has no fish and is the lowest spot on earth. The Sea of Galilee is famous for its fish. It is 211 metres below sea level.

IXθYZ

The fish symbol (above) was used by the early Christians. The Greek word is ichthus. The initials stand for "Jesus Christ, God's Son, Saviour".

DRUSILLA (Hebrew: Learned)

Acts 24:24-27

Drusilla was the wife of Felix the Roman governor. Ironically the Bible mentions her as a Jewish woman *(Acts 24:24)*.

"After some days Felix came with his wife Drusilla, who was Jewish. He sent for Paul and listened to him as he talked about his faith in Christ Jesus".

But the sad part of the episode was the behaviour of Felix. Paul was a prisoner. All sorts of charges were levelled at him by the Jewish elders, who were afraid that Paul would convert many more to Christianity.

Felix and Drusilla were having a first-hand instruction on faith by the master preacher, Paul, who had converted hundreds, or perhaps even thousands, in the Asia Minor region. But all that the brilliant scholar Gamiel of Tarsus said fell on deaf ears. They were corrupt people.

Drusilla, being of Jewish descent, could have nodded her head a few times accepting the faith as stated by Paul, who was arguing his case with the governor. Paul made his defence with great respect to Felix. After he had heard the lengthy defence by Paul, Felix, was afraid and said, "You may leave now. I will call you again when I get the chance".

Felix did not help him in any way at all; neither did Drusilla do anything to help. Two years passed as Paul languished in jail. Porcius Festus succeeded Felix as governor. Felix, it is written, "wanted to gain favour with the Jews so he left Paul in prison". Maybe the Jewish authorities had a hand in making their representation to the governor's wife, who, being Jewish, helped to influence Felix to behave that way. This lady could have used her influence to spread the Christian faith instead of helping the enemy (the Romans).

DUCOIDA (Two Coins Widow)
Mark 12:41-44; Luke 21:1-4

Jesus saw a poor widow drop two coins in the Temple of Jerusalem treasury box as an offering. Jesus was seated near the Court of Women in the Temple from where He had a good view of what was going on. This was a few days before He was arrested and crucified. The Passover was just approaching and there was a good number of people in the Temple. Many of them were rich people who were making large contributions as offerings.

Then came along this poor widow and she took out two copper coins and gave these as her contribution. This act caught the eye of Jesus. He knew that she was a miserably poor woman. What would God want to do with the two miserable copper coins? But it was all she had and Jesus knew this. He called His disciples together and drew their attention to the poor widow and her contribution. "I tell you that this poor widow put in more than all the others. For the others offered their gifts from what they had to spare of their riches; but she, poor as she is, gave all she had to live on".

This incident teaches us a few factors:

1 — God is watching us continuously and knows what we give out as charity or sacrificial offerings.

2 — It is not the size of the offering or the cost of the items given to God that matters; rather it is our sincerity of heart that God wants. He knows our affordability.

3 — Last, but not least, we need to give something to God as an offering. God is not to be viewed as rich or as someone to whom, having everything, nothing need be given.

ELISHEBA
Exodus 6:20-26

She was the daughter of Amminadab and sister of Nahshon. She was Aaron's wife. She bore him Nadab, Abihu, Eleazar, and Ithamar. Aaron and Moses were brothers to whom the Lord said, "Lead the tribes of Israel out of Egypt".

She and the other women of her time formed a group of stalwarts who took part in the great deliverance from Egypt "by the mighty hand of the Lord". They were held captive as slaves and there was no escape. Pharaoh and the Egyptian hierarchy needed them as slaves. In spite of so many difficult times the Lord tested the stubbornness of the Pharaoh, who refused to let them go. She made it, finally, to the Promised Land, after forty years of wandering in the desert.

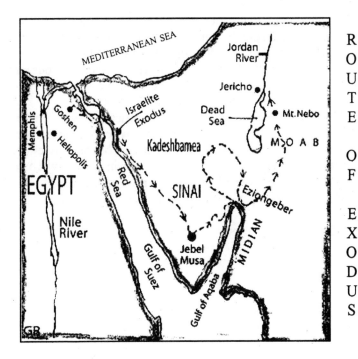

ELIZABETH (Oath of God)
Luke 1:5-45

During the time when Herod was King of Judea, there was a priest named Zechariah, who belonged to the priestly order of Abijah. His wife's name was Elizabeth; she also belonged to a priestly family. They both lived good lives in God's sight and obeyed fully all of the Lord's laws and commands. They had no children because Elizabeth could not have any, and both she and her husband were very old.

One day while Zechariah was doing his Temple duties, an angel appeared and told him that his wife Elizabeth would bear him a son. "You are to name him John".

Sometime later that day, when he went home after completing his duties in the Temple, he was told his wife Elizabeth was pregnant. Elizabeth said, "Now at last the Lord has helped me. He has taken away my public disgrace!"

Zechariah doubted God's mercy to his wife and for this he was temporarily made dumb — till the day the child was born. Elizabeth on the other hand was a lady full of faith in the Lord.

It was also Elizabeth who, at Ain Karim, greeted her cousin Mary with the special words, "You are the most blessed of all women, and blessed is the child you will bear!" (Jesus).

This word blessed has a special significance as it could mean that Mary was greatly favoured by God. When we say someone is blessed with some talents it means the person has been given special talents or privileges. We all have some blessings bestowed on us by God. Let us count our blessings and give praise to Him — from whom all goodness ensues.

ENDORA (Woman of Endor)

1 Samuel 28:3-25

Are there any good witches? Are witches only women? Who is the famous witch in the Bible? Is witchcraft forbidden in all its forms? Wizards are the male counterparts.

The woman I'm going to introduce lived at a very difficult time in the history of Israel. Saul was camped on Mount Gilboa opposite the Philistine camp and was certain of being defeated. He was a very desperate man.

He was so terrified that he asked God for help. "But the Lord did not answer him at all, either by dreams or by the use of Urim and Thummim or by prophets" *(1 Samuel 28:6).*

Saul in his desperation ordered his officials to come and help him: "Find me a woman who is a medium, and I will go and consult her".

The officials were taken aback because this was the same King Saul who had ordered all witches and mediums to be put to death. He had forced the fortune-tellers to leave his kingdom. Now he wanted to consult one about his future.

He was told there was a medium in the town of Endor.

Perhaps that's how Samantha's mother, Endora, got her name in the popular TV series *Bewitched*. Samantha is a beautiful witch who is trying to lead a good life as a normal woman, but one who still has her supernatural powers. Probably, you know that witches and mediums never fared well with the Church. Joan of Arc was branded a witch and burned at the stake. Students of American history learn about the Salem Witch Trial of the nineteenth century. In 1415 Jan Hus, the Czech religious reformer, was burned at the stake by a Catholic council, leading to civil war in Bohemia.

Anyway, here Saul disguised himself and went to meet the woman. She did not recognize him at first. He asked her to summon Samuel, the prophet, to speak to him. At that time Samuel was already long dead and buried in his home town of Ramah.

The woman refused; "Surely you know what King Saul has done ... Why, then, are you trying to trap me and get me killed?"

Saul made a sacred vow and assured her no harm would come to her for helping him. She obliged and summoned Samuel.

When Samuel came he recognized Saul and addressed him as King Saul. Now Saul's identity was out in the open. The woman was frightened to death and screamed and said to Saul, "Why have you tricked me? You are King Saul!"

"Don't be afraid!" Saul answered her.

Samuel, when he appeared, was upset that Saul had disturbed him: "Why have you disturbed me? Why did you make me come back?"

Saul apologized and told him his problems and predicament: "God has abandoned me. He doesn't answer me any more, either by prophets or by dreams".

Samuel then explained what went wrong with Saul's relationship with God. Saul in his anger for and jealousy of David had slaughtered all the holy priests. The priest Ahimelech and all his relatives were killed. One day he had Doeg and his soldiers kill eighty-five priests and other inhabitants of Nob, the city of priests, along with the men, women, children, babes, cattle, donkeys and sheep *(1 Samuel 22:16-19)*. One of Ahimelech's sons, Abiathar escaped and narrated the whole episode to David.

The spirit of Samuel also told Saul of how he and his sons would die and the kingdom would be handed over to David. Saul fell down terrified at the stressful news.

The woman was filled with pity for Saul and said, "Please, sir, I risked my life by doing what you asked. Now please do what I ask. Let me prepare some food for you. You must eat so that you will be strong enough to travel". Saul had not eaten anything, day or night, and he was heartbroken and weak. Finally, after much persuasion, he agreed.

"The woman quickly killed a calf which she had been fattening. Then she took some flour, prepared it, and baked some bread without yeast. She set the food before Saul and his officers and they ate it. And they left that same night".

She was a good woman, even though she was a witch. I would consider her so. There was some real effort on her part to prepare a good meal in a hurry at that hour and under such duress. I don't think for this effort there was any witchcraft. It was real hard work. She could have been content with summoning Samuel from the dead. Then why waste time preparing a meal for the men who would surely be dead in a couple of hours? She cared. This shows she had the heart of a good woman, medium, witch, or whatever else you may wish you call her. She cooked the last supper for the first King of Israel.

Tips for Stress Management:

Let us not be too quick to evaluate and condemn others, whom we may not know well. At times we act as the prosecutor, the judge and the jury.

Read slowly the Bible verses. If your fuse is blown, or if you are threatened by difficult stressors, you will find the words soothing and the trip switch of your panic button will be reset automatically.

Never try black magic or the occult. There are forms of cult techniques and rituals by opportunists. Stay clear off these.

Some forms of Yoga are cults. True Yoga is not.

Try T'ai chi, Aromatherapy or Hydrotherapy. Visualization of Bible stories helps to detoxify a diseased or troubled mind.

ESTHER (Hebrew: Star)
Esther 2:17

Esther was a Jewish orphan. She was raised by her cousin Mordecai. Her Israelite name was Hadassah, meaning myrtle — a sweet-smelling, star-petalled floral plant.

The events of the Book of Esther takes place in the Persia of King Xerxes. They centre round the Jewish heroine, Esther, who showed great courage and wisdom to save her people from extermination by their enemies. All this is celebrated in the Jewish festival of Purim.

King Xerxes of Persia ruled from his capital, Susa, to cover about 127 provinces all the way from India to Ethiopia. He did not get along well with his Queen Vashti. In fact, when the King threw a banquet for all his officials, to celebrate the third year of his reign, the queen did not attend. Instead she threw a rival party.

The king's banquet, to which both the rich and the poor were invited, continued for a whole week. The queen's party on the other hand was only for the women.

On the seventh day the king called his seven eunuchs and ordered them to bring Queen Vashti, wearing her royal crown. The queen heard the king's request but did not come to meet either the king or the guests. The king was furious. He consulted his best advisors. This was their verdict: "Queen Vashti has insulted not only the king but . . . every man in the empire! . . . Wives everywhere will have no respect for their husbands, and husbands will be angry with their wives. If it please Your Majesty, issue a royal proclamation that Vashti may never again appear before the king. . . . Then give her place as queen to some better woman". It was hoped that with this proclamation, "every woman will treat her husband with proper respect, whether he's rich or poor".

The king was further advised to search for a suitable candidate to be queen: ". . . bring all these beautiful young girls to your harem here in Susa. Put them in the care of Hegai, the eunuch . . . and let them be given a beauty treatment". The king thought it was a good idea and went with it.

There were many Jews at that time in Susa, in spite of the thousands who returned to Jerusalem after being released from Babylonic exile. Once before, as you probably know, King Nebuchadnezzar of Babylon took King Jeconiah of Judah into exile from Jerusalem along with thousands of Jews. One of these Jews was Mordecai. He had a cousin named Hadassah (Hebrew name), the daughter of Abigail, and when her parents died Mordecai adopted her and brought her up. One of the girls brought before the eunuch Hegai, was Esther. He liked her because of her beauty. He lost no time in giving her the beauty treatment of massage and special diet. He even assigned seven young girls to serve her. On the advice of Mordecai Esther kept it a secret that she was a Jew. Mordecai would walk every day to the courtyard to see how she was progressing.

The beauty treatment and special diet took a year for Esther as she was very slim. Finally, the time came for Esther to go before the king. The king earlier had viewed one by one all the other girls and still felt unhappy. When Esther appeared before the king, he "liked her more than any of the other girls". The king placed the royal crown on her head and made her queen. The king held a great banquet in honour of Esther and invited all his officials and administrators. He also proclaimed that day a holiday for the whole empire and distributed gifts to one and all.

Mordecai managed to gain an important position in the palace, thanks also to Queen Esther. Two eunuchs in the palace, Bigthana and Teresh became hostile to King Xerxes and planned to assassinate him. Mordecai found out about this and told Esther, who told the king. After investigations they were found guilty and hanged.

In the king's court was Haman, the prime minister, who had special status. He was an Agagite — a people who had been traditional enemies of the Israelites.

Everyone was supposed to bow before him out of homage by a special decree of the king. Mordecai refused to bow before him because, he declared, "I am a Jew". Hamam was furious when he heard it and vowed to punish Mordecai and kill every Jew in the Persian Empire.

Haman managed to win the king's favour and convinced him of the necessity to exterminate all the Jews. A proclamation declared that this was to take place on the 13th day of the month of Adar.

Throughout the provinces the news brought sorrow. There was loud mourning among the Jews. They fasted, wept, wailed and most of them put on sackcloth and covered their faces with ash. Soon Esther came to know about the proclamation. She decided to do something about it.

"Go and gather all the Jews in Susa together; hold a fast and pray for me. Don't eat or drink anything for days and three nights. My servant-girls and I will be doing the same. After that, I will go to the king." . . .

Esther approached the king: "If it please Your Majesty, I would like you and Haman to be my guests tonight at a banquet I am preparing for you".

Queen Esther had two days of banquet for the king and Haman. The prime minister was very happy with the queen and the honour she gave him. But when he saw Mordecai the Jew he was upset. He decided to build special gallows — on the advice of his wife, Zeresh.

The king, meanwhile, was finding ways to reward Mordecai for saving his life. So he asked Haman what he should do to the one "I wish very much to honour". Haman thought that this was a special chance to get more honour for himself.

"Order royal robes to be brought for this man — robes that you yourself wear. Order a royal crown to be put on your own horse. Then get one of your highest noblemen to dress the man in these robes and lead him mounted on the horse, through the city square. Let the nobleman announce as they go: 'See how the king rewards a man he wishes to honour!'".

Then the king said to Haman, "Hurry and get the robes and the horse, and provide these honours for Mordecai the Jew. Do everything for him that you suggested. You will find him sitting at the entrance of the palace. Haman was very stressed and disappointed but could not displease the king. So Haman led Mordecai through the streets with full honours. Then, having done this, he went back and cried his heart out to his wife. She was determined that Mordecai must be destroyed and encouraged him.

Meanwhile, the king — extremely happy with Esther — asked her to name any favour she wanted, even if it were half the empire.

Then Esther asked for this favour — that her people be spared, and pointed out that Haman was an evil man. The king was shocked at all these revelations. He went to meditate in the palace garden.

Haman realized that the king would punish him because of Esther's influence.

Haman threw himself at Esther's feet and begged her for mercy. When Esther went to her couch, Haman leaned on her — begging her for his life. The king came into the room and, seeing the sight, he cried out, "Is this man going to rape the queen right here in front of me, in my own palace?"

Then he heard from one of the royal eunuchs that Haman had built the seventy-five-foot-high gallows to hang Mordecai. "Hang Haman on it!" the king commanded.

That same day King Xerxes gave Queen Esther all the property of Haman after he was hanged on the same gallows. The Jews were allowed to defend themselves if they were attacked — due to the royal proclamation that could not be revoked. The Jews became victorious over their enemies.

Esther made a command that the Jewish people for all time should celebrate the feast of Purim. Purim meant lots that were cast to choose the day to exterminate all the Jews. This feast is observed with fasting and penance on the fourteenth and fifteenth days of Adar, as special holidays.

Quotable Quote:

You may part with something beautiful, rare and even costly, but never part with anything that is holy. Without holiness you can never hope to be in the company of God.

Dr G. Reth

EUNICE (Good Victory)
Acts 16:1

Eunice was Jewish and a believer. Her father was Greek. Her son was Timothy, a devotee of Jesus Christ through the Apostle Paul.

The family lived in Lystra in the hill country of modern-day Turkey. It was in Lystra that Paul and Barnabas were hailed as gods after they healed a known cripple. They were also stoned by an angry mob there. This, thus, was a difficult city for preachers. Yet it was there that Timothy was born and where he gave witness to Our Lord Jesus. Eunice named her son Timothy (one who honours God — and that is what he did).

In the Bible we read of two important Letters written by St Paul to Timothy. This young lad became a faithful companion of the Apostle Paul in his missionary work. The first Letter to Timothy deals with three main concerns:

It is a warning against false teaching in the Early Church. (At that time there were problems arising from Jewish ideology.)

There are specific instructions about Church administration, worship, and character building.

It contains advice to Timothy to be a good missionary of Our Lord Jesus, and discusses his responsibilities

The second Letter deals with advice from Paul to Timothy, whom he regards as a personal assistant. The theme of the Letter is endurance.

Eunice should be very proud of such a son.

EVE (Hebrew: Life-giving)
Genesis 2:23

The name of the first woman in Paradise, in a place called Eden, was Woman (meaning made from man). Later, after she had committed the sin of disobedience, she was named Eve *(Genesis 3:20)*.

Adam named her Eve (the name sounds similar to the Hebrew word for living) because she was the mother of all human beings (except him, of course). She was a special creature created by God out of human male parts. Adam, the first man, was created from clay.

In fact, in the middle of Chapter 2 of Genesis, verse 21, we learn that God made the man fall into a deep sleep. This was a form of anaesthesia. Then God took out one of the ribs of the man and closed up the flesh. He formed a woman out of the rib and brought her to him. Then the man said, "At last, here is one of my own kind — Bone taken from my bone, and flesh from my flesh. 'Woman' is her name because she was taken out of man".

This is the only case in human history when a man "gave birth" to a woman, that is woman was created out of a man by a special form of cloning.

In the perfect form, the woman was happy and all was well. But even in Paradise the woman was discontented. She could be tempted and could tempt others — like her husband, Adam. Everything was not perfect in Paradise. There was evil. This was in the form of a creature — the snake which could tempt the woman, and coax her to commit the sin of disobedience. The sin was to eat of the fruit of the Tree of Knowledge of Good and Bad.

"God told us," she declared to the evil voice of the creature, "not to eat the fruit of that tree or even touch it; if we do, we will die". But one of the irresistible attributes of women is intense curiosity. She succumbed to it.

The woman saw how beautiful the tree was and how good its fruit would be to eat, and thought wrong. What was this thought disorder? She thought "How wonderful it would be to become wise" *(Genesis 3:6)*.

When God asked Adam, "Did you eat the fruit that I told you not to eat?" the man answered, "The woman you put here with me gave me the fruit, and I ate it". Adam clearly wanted to convey the message that it was only because of "the woman you put here". He knew he did wrong and he wanted to blame it on someone. Instead of a simple, "Yes, I ate it," he was looking for an excuse. It happens even now — all the time. It is man's second nature.

Then the Lord asked the woman, "Why did you do this?" He wanted to show how vulnerable she was to trickery. She could have said, "Curiosity," instead she passed the buck and blamed the evil creature. "The snake tricked me into eating it".

Then came the famous judgement in Paradise, when God took all the comforts and privileges from the humans. "You will have to work hard and sweat to make the soil produce anything, until you go back to the soil from which you were formed. You were made from soil, and you will become soil again".

It is immediately after this sentence and judgement that we learn the new name of the woman in Paradise, namely Eve. "Adam named his wife Eve, because she was the mother of all humans beings". They were then expelled from Paradise. The children of Eve were: Cain and Able and Seth (a replacement, meaning a person to take the place of Abel who was killed). Her great sorrows included the death of her younger son, killed by her first-born, who became the first murderer. "When Adam was 130 years old, he had a son who was like him, and he named him Seth". Adam and Eve had other children and Adam died at the age of 930 *(Genesis 5:4,5).*

Cain and his wife had a son Enoch. Enoch had a son Irad, Irad had a son Mehujael. Mehujael had a son Methushuel. Methushuel had a son Lamech. Lamech had two wives, Adah and Zillah. Adah gave birth to two sons Jabal — the ancestor of those who raise livestock and live in tents — and Jubal — the ancestor of musicians. Zillah gave birth to Tubal Cain, who is regarded as the ancestor of metal-tool workers, and his sister Naamah.

Think It Over:

Blaming the other party or person is a very old practice. It existed even in Paradise. Adam blamed Eve and she in turn blamed the serpent. Maybe the serpent, if questioned, would have blamed it on something.

Sometime or other we need to get over the habit of blaming someone or something for our mistakes. Accept the blame. To err is human. To forgive is divine. To admit an error is to be humble.

FIERA (Fiery)
Matthew 26:69-75; Mark 14, 66-72

She was the girl who was present near the charcoal fire that was kept going to keep the people warm in the courtyard of the High Priest's house.

Simon Peter and another disciple followed Jesus. The other disciple was well known to the High Priest, so he went with Jesus into the courtyard. Peter remained outside the gate *(John 18:15-16)*. This disciple went out and spoke to the girl at the gate and brought Peter in.

This indicated that the entrance into the courtyard of the High Priest was restricted. People were screened before they were let in. This is the reason the other apostles and disciples did not go along in the entourage that followed Jesus into the High Priest's house. Peter was bold enough to go along knowing that there was danger in being associated with Jesus, who had just been arrested. There is no mention of the identity of the disciple who seemed to be rather well known to the High Priest and also, we presume, to the gate keeper, who happened to be a woman.

This girl at the gate said to Peter, "Aren't you also one of the disciples of that man?" *(John 18:17)*.

Peter answered, "No, I am not".

In Mark's Gospel *(14: 66-72)* we learn of this incident vividly. She is described as one of the servants of the High Priest: "When she saw Peter warming himself, she looked straight at him and said, "You, too, were with Jesus of Nazareth". Peter denied it. Just then the cock crowed.

The servant woman saw him there and began to repeat to the bystanders, "He is one of them!" *(Mark 14:69-72)*. She tried to win the support of the others to fix Peter as a collaborator. But, Peter denied it vehemently.

"I swear that I am telling the truth! May God punish me if I am not! I do not know the man you are talking about!" Immediately the cock crowed a second time. Peter remembered the words of Jesus and wept bitterly.

Jesus is the Lamb of God. He was led away like a lamb to the slaughterhouse.

Think It Over:

There are many, many times when you have denied God the respect and gratitude that the Creator deserves.

There are many more times when you have insulted God and even cursed the Almighty. How merciful is God, who let you off the hook without punishing you.

The Lamb:

Sheep are mentioned more than 400 times in the Bible. Why? Because this animal:

1 — Is the Paschal Lamb.

2 — Exhibits meek and quiet virtues.

3 — Very often is offered in sacrifice to God for sins to be forgiven.

4 — Provides wool — a very expensive fibre for clothing and rugs.

5 — Provides skins, which may be used for tents, shoes and clothing.

6 — Provides milk for use in daily cooking and feeding.

7 — Provides meat, which is highly prized and is consumed only on special occasions.

GOMER (Hebrew: Complete)
Hosea 1:3

There are very few stories to rival this Biblical story. It is a very uncommon story even today. It is so rare that there are Biblical scholars even today who doubt it took place at all. But, when you read between the lines you will see that it can happen.

Now, what is all this fuss? Who was Gomer? What is the "completeness" in the story? Gomer was a fun-loving, beautiful prostitute — an unfaithful wife. She is the symbol of fun-seekers who form the women of the night in the major cities of the world. Offer them help to come out of this risky flesh trade and they refuse it. They love danger with all its frills. Perhaps it was different in primitive times — when they did not know about HIV or AIDS or herpes or syphilis or gonorrhoea or chlamydia or even hepatitis B. All these can be easily contracted from prostitutes.

I went for an advanced course in sexually transmitted diseases in Bangkok. One of the delights in the sightseeing tours of Bangkok is to visit the Pat Pong District. What is so special about this place, one would wonder? — It is the red-light district, the Soho of the East. Here you will see all sorts of sex-trade-related activities. Homosexuals are available; lesbians; young girls; boys; sex toys; videos, VCD and DVD that are triple-X rated; and so on. There are even animals for sexual fantasies. It's like Sodom and Gomorrah.

One can interview and see young, pretty girls offering themselves for sale. As a physician I had several come to the registered clinic. To the question, "Why do you want to adopt this dangerous lifestyle?" they reply dismissively it with silly excuses. It is not only in Bangkok; it is the same everywhere.

You probably know of such individuals in your town or city. Have you seen the movie *Pretty Woman*, starring Julia Roberts?

Anyway, coming back to the story, Gomer was (like Israel at that time) an adulteress, a prostitute. Yet God loved Israel, despite her sinning ways. God told a very holy and upright man, Hosea, to go and marry Gomer.

"Go and get married; your wife will be unfaithful, and your children will be just like her. In the same way, my people have left me and become unfaithful" *(Hosea 1:2)*. Hosea is known in many churches for that famous hymn:

"Come back to me with all your heart,
Don't let fear keep us apart.
Trees do bend, though straight and tall
So must we to others call. . . .
Long have I waited for your coming home . . ."

In sincere humility and obedience Hosea married Gomer. It must have been a difficult marriage with such a wayward woman. Yet she bore him two sons and a daughter, before leaving the good man for the flesh trade.

What could be the other reasons for leaving a faithful, sincere, religious man? Perhaps it was a desire to seek more adventures and greener pastures. Hosea must have appealed to her as a priestly, holy man. She was the opposite in her likes and dislikes.

Now, we have something interesting. God intervenes. God told Hosea, "Go again and show your love for a woman who is committing adultery with a lover. You must love her just as I still love the people of Israel." . . .

So, poor Hosea went in search of his wife to all the red-light areas and found her. He had to pay fifteen pieces of silver and seven bushels of barley to buy her from her lover. Then he told her that she would "have to wait for me without being a prostitute or committing adultery". This meant she had to live with him and he wanted her to live with him and be his wife for a long period of time. Probably she respected his sincerity and gave up her sinful ways.

Motivation and the Blues:

Adversity will continue to exist in spite of material wealth and technological progress. Welcome and tolerate some adversity. It is the fire test to bring out the colour, refiness and true character.

Dr G. Reth

69

HAGAR (Flight)
Genesis 16:15

God's ways are not our ways. It is impossible to comprehend the mind of God. Abraham and Sarai (her later name was Sarah) were a rich couple and well advanced in years. Their family life was lacking in one area — children. They were childless. Abraham's wife, out of frustration at her infertility (or barrenness), decided to give her servant or slave, Hagar, to Abraham. This is surrogate pregnancy — make no mistake about it. Abraham was obviously happy about it. Hagar probably had no choice, as servants in those days were slaves. A rich person owned them body and soul. You could do anything with them. Hagar was one such person — no family, no relatives and no personality. Her name says it all — run, fly, vamoose, or get lost.

She became pregnant and incurred the wrath of Sarai. Maybe she had morning sickness. Maybe she could not do much of her regular duties. Maybe she relaxed. We can't judge her roughly. Historically, she had a bad record. Not many scholars liked her. She was a nobody — not from any great family. She was an Egyptian slave or a bedouin servant. Whatever her background God was very merciful to her. God in His kindness came directly to help her when Sarai had the pregnant Hagar driven into the desert, perhaps to die. (The Bible says Sarai treated her cruelly so she ran away.) There the angel of the Lord met her near a spring and told her to go back to her mistress and submit to her *(Genesis 16:9)*. She was also told that she would have a son and she was to name the boy Ishmael. This is a special name given by God. The name means 'God will hear' — because God "heard your cry of distress".

"I will give you so many descendants that no one will be able to count them. . . . your son will live like a wild donkey; he will be against everyone, and everyone will be against him".

This certainly is very unfair. Nobody should be condemned this way — for no sin of his own. But in life we do encounter people with handicaps. Others make fun of them. "Blessed are you when men revile you and persecute you". Remember the words of the

Beatitudes. Your gift is in Heaven. In fact all those who are handicapped, or are unfortunate in this world, already have high points in Heaven. God loves you more.

So Hagar went back to her mistress and Abraham. The baby was born and was named Ishmael. Abraham, known at that time as Abram, was eighty-six years old.

When Abraham was ninety-nine years old, the Lord appeared to him and made a covenant with him: "Your name will be no longer be Abram but Abraham (ancestor of many nations). . . . I will keep my promise to you and to your descendants in future generations."
. . . He was also told to have the circumcision ritual for all males. So Abraham and Ishmael were circumcised on the same day. He was ninety-nine and Ishmael was thirteen years old.

He also asked God if Ishmael could be his heir. But God replied, "No. Your wife Sarah will bear you a son and you will name him Isaac [Hebrew: he laughs]. I will keep my covenant with him and with his descendants for ever. . . . He will be the father of twelve princes." . . . God also changed Sara's name to Sarah (princess).

Sarah and Abraham were visited by three angels *(Genesis 18:1-18)*. These men accepted Abraham's hospitality and told them the good news that Sarah would have a baby boy in nine months time. Sarah laughed, "Now that I am old and worn out, can I still enjoy sex? And besides, my husband is old too".

When Isaac was born Abraham was one hundred years old. Sarah was a very happy woman but terribly unhappy with Hagar. She could not tolerate Ishmael playing with Isaac. "Send this slave-girl and her son away. The son of this woman must not get any part of your wealth, which my son Isaac should inherit".

Next morning Abraham gave Hagar some food and a leather bag full of water, then he sent the mother and child away. She left and wandered in the wilderness of Beersheba. When all the water was exhausted, she left the child under a bush and sat down and cried out to the Lord, "I can't bear to see my child die". Hearing her cries the child started crying. God heard their cries and spoke to them through an angel.

When she opened her eyes she saw a well. She filled the leather bag with water and gave some to the boy. The boy grew up and became a skilful hunter. His mother got him an Egyptian wife. The modern-day Egyptians and many Palestine people consider themselves to be descendants of Ishmael.

The well at Beersheba (the Well of the Vow) is the Zamzam Well considered as the holy well of the Muslim pilgrims at Mecca.

But Beersheba in reality is in Judah, about twenty kilometres from Hebron, where Abraham and Sarah lived and are buried.

It is my contention that Abraham left his home town of Ur (of the Chaldees, in Iraq) to settle down in Haran initially. He later moved to Canaan, the land promised to him by God. He moved finally to Beersheba. The travel along the Fertile Crescent from Ur to Beersheba is just over 1,500 km. It is better to go along the fertile stretch rather than the direct route because of the hostile desert. The well where Hagar received water for herself and her child is not in Saudi Arabia or specifically Mecca. It is in Beersheba in present-day Israel. The well is still there. Hagar went there because she had run away to the same place once before — when she could not get along with Sarah. The angel told her to go back to Sarah and Abraham. Her son Ishmael is believed to be the ancestor of the Muslims.

Abraham's journey was westwards. He also lived in Kadesh near Beersheba and in Mamre, Shur and Gerar. It was to King Abimelech of Gerar that he lied about Sarah being his sister when in reality she was his wife. He paid 400 pieces of silver for a plot near Mamre, in Hebron as a burial ground. This included the Machpelah Cave.

HANNAH (Hebrew: Grace)

1 Samuel 1:1-23

The scene in Ramah of the hill country of Ephraim. Hers is a study of depression and how to overcome it. In her case the remedy was grace. She experienced the miracle-working, divine amazing grace, and that is something we ought to look forward to.

Q. What is grace?

A. The Scott Foresman Advanced Dictionary defines it as beauty of form, charm, goodwill, favour, mercy or pardon, favour and love of God.

Grace is a blessing bestowed by God on one who earns the honour. "Hail Mary full of Grace," was the salutation by Angel Gabriel to Mary who was highly favoured by God.

In this case Hannah in her unfortunate status won God's favour, and became very fortunate.

She was the wife of Elkanah. He had another wife, Peninnah — who was very rude. Hannah had no children and the other woman had many children. Both lived in the same house. You can imagine the conversation that went on in that home. It was a case of the fortunate teasing the unfortunate. With no proper education, in those primitive times it must have been horrible day and night.

Whenever Hannah went up to the house of the Lord, her rival (the other wife) provoked her (with comments) till she wept and would not eat *(1 Samuel 1:7)*.

Every year Elkanah went from Ramah to worship and offer sacrifices to the Almighty, as the shrine of the Ark of the Covenant was in Shiloh.

Hophni and Phinehas the two sons of Eli, were priests of the Lord. Elkanah, while offering the meat for sacrifice, would give one share to Peninnah and another to each of her children. He would give a small fraction to Hannah "because the Lord had kept her from having children". This went on year after year. When Hannah cried her heart out at the humiliation, her husband would ask her, "Hannah, why are you crying? Why won't you eat? Why are you always so sad? Don't I mean to you more than ten sons?"

During one visit she could contain her sorrow no more so she cried bitterly to the Lord, "Almighty Lord, look at me, your servant! See my trouble and remember me! Don't forget me! If you give me a son, I promise that I will dedicate him to you for his whole life and that he will never have his hair cut".

Eli, the priest watched her pray. Her lips moved and there was no sound. So Eli thought that she was drunk and he said to her, "Stop making a drunken show of yourself! Stop, your drinking and sober up!" he ordered, as he observed her swaying.

"No, I'm not drunk, sir," she answered. "I haven't been drinking! I am desperate, and I have been praying, pouring out my troubles to the Lord. Don't think I am a worthless woman. I have been praying like this because I'm so miserable".

"Go in peace," Eli said, "and may the God of Israel give you what you have asked for".

"May you always think kindly of me," she replied and left.

That same year she got pregnant and delivered a son, who came to be one of the greatest men in Israel's history. His name was Samuel. (The name in Hebrew means 'name of God', in this case with the connotation 'I asked'.)

But, in that same year of the birth she did not go to the shrine at Shiloh to give thanks with her husband and his other wife and children. They left without her because she chose not to go.

She said she would take him to the temple with gifts after she had weaned him. So they went and Hannah stayed at home and nursed the child.

After the child was weaned she took him to Shiloh, along with a three-year-old bull calf, a bushel of flour and a leather bag full of wine. They killed the bull then took the child to Eli, the priest. She asked him, "Excuse me, sir. Do you remember me?" Then she refreshed his memory by recounting the incident of her last meeting with the old priest. "I asked [God] for this child, and He gave me what I asked for. So I am dedicating him to the Lord. As long as he lives, he will belong to the Lord". From that time onwards young Samuel lived in the shrine with Eli.

It is wonderful that Hannah, a barren, ridiculed woman, was made fortunate this way, but God rewarded her faith further by giving her seven children — including three more sons, besides Samuel.

Today we have Hannah's prayer of thanksgiving and praise *(1 Samuel 2:1-11)*, and it has all the features similar to the Magnificat. It begins with:

"The Lord has filled my heart with joy;
how happy I am because of what He has done!
I laugh at my enemies;
how joyful I am because God has helped me!"

Each year, the Bible says, Hannah would go up to Shiloh and give Samuel a new linen apron robe *(1 Samuel 2:19)*. Eli would bless her and Elkanah saying, "May the Lord give you other children by this woman to take the place of the one you dedicated to Him".

The Ark of the Covenant:

The Ark of the Covenant at Shiloh was lost to the Philistines. It was returned miraculously to the Israelites without a war or peace agreement.

75

HAPI (Happiness)
Luke 11:27-28

Jesus was performing miracles and doing good deeds of mercy in public ministry. He was the embodiment of goodness. Clearly, anyone could see for themselves what a wonderful person Jesus was. A certain woman in the crowd could not contain her admiration for Him.

She spoke from the crowd, "How happy is the woman who bore you and nursed you!" This was the reference to Mary, the mother of Jesus. A mother would be proud to have a son such as Jesus. Instead of complimenting her, Jesus modestly told Hapi that true happiness is when people hear the Word of God and keep it or obey it. God is happy when we do what God wants us to do.

Mary, the mother of Jesus, is rarely portrayed in pictures or statues as a happy, smiling woman. Very often the expression on her face is that of a sorrowful mother. There is even a popular church in Penang, Malaysia, with the title Mother of Sorrows. The expression of the Virgin of Guadalupe is that of a very sad lady. The face of our Lady of Perpetual Succour is also one of a sorrowful lady. The popular hymn sung at the Redemptorists' Novena is based on that painting of a sad and apprehensive face. The tragic events of the crucifixion and sufferings are all portrayed on her face.

But I still think she was happy to be the mother of the Saviour. She is the happy girl who sang her praises with the Magnificat. This song of joy is the passage from Luke's Gospel. It gives us a good insight into the mind of Mary. She had an opinion that God was a just and loving person who loved the underprivileged more.

HERODIAS (Heroic)

Mark 6:18-19

She was King Herod's brother's wife (i.e. Philip's wife). She had a daughter named Salome.

Philip was the ruler of the territory of Iturea and Trachonitis. He was a mean man, so it was convenient for Herodias to go over to King Herod Antipas, the ruler of Galilee. She was married to him though she was still legally married to Philip. This was a crime in the eyes of John the Baptist. Whenever John made this sin known in his discourses it was an embarrassment to Herodias. She then plotted against John because she bore a grudge against him. Herodias could not kill him because of Herod's fear of him — as a holy man.

The chance came on Herod's birthday, when he threw a grand feast for all the *crème de la crème* of Jerusalem. John was put in jail because of his accusations of her adultery. Herodias asked her daughter to dance to please Herod. He was so pleased that he asked her what she wanted. He was willing to give her even half his kingdom.

The girl asked her mother and she replied, ". . . the head of John the Baptist on a dish". Salome made this demand to the king. The king was visibly worried and almost refused the request. He had to save his name before so many dignitaries, so he granted Salome's request. John was beheaded. What a waste of a good man's life! John did not deserve to end his good life in this manner. Herodias was a wicked woman, an adulteress, and a bad mother to give such an example of evil to her young daughter, Salome.

This is an example of the axiom 'A bad tree bears bad fruit'. Herodias had the good fortune to be somebody powerful in high society. She could have brought up her daughter right with good virtues.

John was a special person, a man of God. He was the cousin of Jesus. His mother was Elizabeth — the aged cousin of Mary, mother of Jesus.

HULDAH (Gliding, Fleeting, also Weasel)
2 Kings 22:14

The root word could be from the quick action movements of animals.

King Josiah of Judah was eight years old when he became king. He ruled Jerusalem as a good king for thirty-one years. Whatever King Josiah did was pleasing to God. He did away with pagan worship which was common all over Israel. His mother was Jedidah, the daughter of Adaiah, from Bozkath.

In order to do the right things he asked the Temple officials and High Priest to read to him the book of the Law in the Temple. He was shocked to note that much of what was written was not practised. He tore his clothes in disappointment and sent the officials to consult the prophetess Huldah.

She lived in the newer part of Jerusalem and was a very pious woman. Her husband was Shallum, the son of Tikvah. He was in charge of the temple robes. She was told about the intentions of the king — how he planned to get rid of pagan worship. She told them to go with this message from the Lord to the king, "I am going to punish Jerusalem and all its people, as written in the book. . . . They have rejected me and have offered sacrifices to other gods . . ." She also told him that, since he was a good king, the punishment to Jerusalem would not come during his reign of thirty-one years.

Josiah's wife was Hamutal, the daughter of Jeremiah, from the city of Libnah. His son Joahaz became king after him. But, he ruled for only three months — as King Neco of Egypt took him as prisoner to Egypt. He was just the opposite of his father, Josiah.

Josiah's other son, Eliakim, was made king by King Neco, with a new name — Jehoiakim. His mother was Zebidah, the daughter of Pedaiah, from the town of Rumah. This king encouraged pagan worship while he ruled as king for eleven years. King Nebuchadnezzar of Babylonia invaded Judah. His son Jehoiachin, his mother Nehushta, family members and others were taken into Babylonic captivity as slaves.

Nebuchadnezzar made Jehoiachin's uncle King of Judah, with

the changed name Zedekiah. His mother was Hamutal, the daughter of Jeremiah of the city of Libnah. He ruled Jerusalem for eleven years. This King also angered God very much with his sinful ways. King Nebuchadnezzar came with an army, captured the king, blinded him and put his sons to death. Then he took him in chains with others to Babylon.

The next King of Babylon, King Evilmerodach, released King Jehoiachin from prison after thirty-seven years of captivity. He permitted him to sit and dine with him, and gave him an allowance.

Huldah, lived during a difficult time in Israelite history. She was the mouthpiece of God. She knew and foretold the destruction of the Temple and God's wrath against the pagan worshippers, but, because Josiah was good, God spared the people during his reign. After that it was just a swift, downward slide to tragedy.

The Temple of Jerusalem (see page 23):

The plot of land was purchased by King David.

It was David's wish to unite all the tribes of the Israelites and give them one capital city. The Ark of the Covenant, he felt, needed a permanent resting site and this would be in the Temple of Jerusalem. Solomon built it in 970-931 BC. The Temple was first destroyed by Nebuchadnezzar, in 587 BC.

The new Temple was rebuilt after the Edict of Cyrus in 538 BC. Herod the Great rebuilt it during his reign (37 BC-4 BC). It was destroyed by the Roman General Titus in AD 70. Now, only the Western Wall remains.

Gad was David's prophet, who told him to "Go up to Araunah's threshing-place and build an altar to the Lord". Araunah did not want to make a huge profit, so he charged a token fee of fifty pieces of silver. Araunah was a Jebusite.

JAEL (Hebrew: Wild Goat)
Judges 4:17-23

The Book of Judges is a compilation of incidents and stories that happened during a period of lawlessness in Israel. This was after the invasion of Canaan and before monarchy was established.

The word Judges is not used in the legal terminology but to describe national heroes. There was civil war and great disloyalty to the True God, who delivered them from slavery in Egypt.

"The people of Israel forgot the Lord their God; they sinned against Him and worshipped the idols of Baal and Asherah" *(Judges 3:7).*

The Lord was very angry with Israel and allowed King Cushan Rishathaim of Mesopotamia to conquer them and rule over them for eight years. The Lord had pity when they cried out for deliverance and sent Othniel, son of Caleb's younger brother Kenaz. Everything went well for a while.

Then once again the people of Israel sinned. The Lord allowed King Eglon of Moab to rule them with the aid of Ammonites and Amalekites. They were subjected to eighteen years of suffering. In answer to their cries for help, the Lord sent the left-handed Ehud, son of Gera to free them. After Ehud's reign, the people sinned again with human sacrifice and pagan worship. This time the Lord allowed them to be conquered by the Canaanite, King Jabin, who was the ruler of Hazor. He had a very able commander named Sisera, a fierce warrior; Jabin with Sisera ruled Israel for twenty years.

The people cried out for help and this time it was a woman, Deborah, the prophetess, as well as the Judge who helped. She sent for Barak to lead the people of Israel.

Heber, the Kenite had his tent close to Kedesh. He moved away from the other Kenites — the descendants of Hobab, the brother-in-law of Moses. Heber's wife was Jael.

Sisera at that time was fleeing from the battle at the foot of Mount Tabor. He saw a tent and a pretty woman there. It was Jael. He imagined she was another simple woman.

"Come in, sir; come into my tent," she invited. "Don't be afraid," she reassured him.

"Please give me a drink of water; I'm thirsty," Sisera told her. She appeared so kind. Jael then opened a leather bag filled with milk and gave him a drink. She then hid him behind a curtain. Everything seemed perfect.

He spoke to her, "Stand at the door of the tent and if anyone comes and asks you if someone is here, say no".

Sisera, being very tired, soon fell asleep. As he lay asleep Jael took a hammer and peg and killed him. Shortly afterwards Barak came along looking for Sisera. Jael told him, "Come here! I'll show you the man you're looking for".

Jael killed the commander of the enemy. The battle was over as the news caused the enemy forces to surrender.

Mount Tabor:

Mount Tabor rises impressively from the fields of the Jezreel Valley in Galilee. It is the site of the Transfiguration (Matthew 17:1-9, Luke 9:28-36, Mark 9:2-8). On this occasion Jesus was seen speaking to the prophets Moses and Elijah. There is a Franciscan basilica and a Greek Orthodox church built there to commemorate the event. There is an excellent road leading to the summit. There were five failed Holy Crusades to capture the sacred spot on this mountain. The Islamic forces then withdrew voluntarily.

JEHOSHEBA (Jehovah's Oath)

2 Chronicles 22:11

Jehosheba was a princess, the daughter of Judah's King Jehoram. Her grandfather was Jehoshaphat, a God-fearing man, but her father was an evil king. Her father murdered all his brothers so that his position would be secure. King Ahab's daughter was the mother of Jehosheba.

Princess Jehosheba was married to a Temple official who was an upright man in the Lord's service, named Jehoiada. All of Jehosheba's older brothers were killed. Her youngest brother Ahaziah escaped. He became the king, but an evil one, for only one year.

Jehosheba was one good princess in a world that was corrupt and wallowing in pagan worship. She took care of her infant nephew Joash. This was Ahaziah's baby. The boy was brought up in the Temple of Jerusalem. She and her husband trained the future King of Judah in the right way. After their death the king listened to wrong advisers.

The princess lived true to her name. She was sworn to God's oath to uphold God's holy name. She could have captured the throne and ruled, as she had all the qualifications — in fact better ones than the evil Athaliah. Very rarely in life we come across such a rare gem.

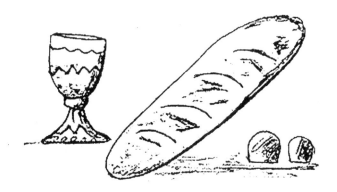

JEPHTHALI (Jephthah's Daughter)
Judges 10:6-18; 11:34-40

One of the saddest episodes in the Bible concerns a pretty dancer who was Jephthah's daughter. She loved music and loved to dance to the music of the tambourine. She was his only child.

Jephthah loved her very much and missed her every time he left home on his battle 'errands'. At that time the Ammonites were at war with the Israelites and Jephthah, the son of Gilead, was known as a mighty warrior and a man of valour. He was also known as a soldier of fortune among the people.

Jephthah's father, Gilead, had many wives and so he had many brothers and sisters. They did not approve of him because his mother was different. He thus did not get any inheritance from his father. The brothers drove him out and he went to live in the Land of Tob. While living away from his people he managed to attract "a group of worthless men, and they went round with him". This is why he was looked upon as a soldier of fortune.

During this time in Israel, the Ammonites were continually at war with Israel. There was no real warrior or champion to fight the many enemies of Israel. God was angry with the Israelites for worshipping other gods.

"Go and cry out to the gods you have chosen. Let them rescue you when you get into trouble," God told the people *(Judges 10:14)*.

The Israelites decided to pray to the real God and ask for forgiveness. They also realized it was time they engaged Jephthah for his help. But he was upset and asked them: "You hated me so much that you forced me to leave my father's house. Why come to me now that you're in trouble?"

Then he gave them a proposal that he should be declared a ruler and then he would be in a position to negotiate with the warring kings. In this capacity he sent a message to the King of Ammon, with whom the Israelites had an outstanding quarrel about land-stealing. The King of Ammon wanted the land given back to him. There was a stalemate and war was the only solution.

Jephthah promised the Lord, "If you give me victory over the

Ammonites, I will burn as an offering the first person that comes out of my house to meet me, when I come back from the victory. I will offer that person to you as a sacrifice" *(Judges 11:30-31)*.

The war stretched on to twenty cities and all the Ammonites were defeated. The rejoicing ruler with his entourage went to the royal house at Mizpah where he lived. The sound of their returning home victorious was sweet music to everyone. The first person who came out dancing with the tambourine was his sweet daughter, Jephthali. Normally, any father would be proud to hug and kiss such a daughter, who came out joyfully to greet him. But, alas, Jephthah was overcome with such sadness at the sight of the dancing, happy girl that he shouted in agony and tore his garments. He said, "Oh, my daughter! You are breaking my heart! Why must it be you that causes me pain? I have made a solemn promise to the Lord, and I cannot take it back!" And he cried his heart out and all the people came to console him. He was an upright man and a God-fearing man so he had to keep his word to God.

The unfortunate girl consoled her father, "If you have made a promise to the Lord, do what you said you would do to me, since the Lord has given you revenge on your enemies, the Ammonites".

Then she asked her father for a favour: "Do this one thing for me. Leave me alone for two months, so that I can go with my friends to wander in the mountains and grieve that I must die a virgin." He granted her this favour.

She must have been quite a young lady to speak such words. Two months later she returned, as promised, to be offered as a human sacrifice for the victory.

This incident is remembered for generations and it is customary for the Israelite women to go out for four days every year to grieve for the daughter of Jephthah of Gilead *(Judges 11:39-40)*.

JEZEBEL (Hebrew: Devotee of the Prince Baal)

1 Kings 16:31

Jezebel was a foreigner (non-Israelite). She was a Phoenician princess, being the daughter of a Sidonian — King Ethbaal. She was married to Samaritan King Ahab, who was an evil man.

There was never anyone else who had devoted himself so completely to doing wrong in the Lord's sight as Ahab — all at the urging of his wife, Jezebel. He committed the most shameful sins.

In the thirty-first year of the reign of King Asa of Judah, Omri became king and ruled for twelve years. The first six years he ruled in Tirzah and he bought the hill estate nearby and called it Samaria in honour of Shemer, from whom he bought the property for six thousand pieces of silver. Omri sinned against the Lord by leading the people astray into idolatry. Ahab was no better. King Ahab, son of Omri, became King of Israel and ruled Samaria for twenty-two years. Ahab built a Temple to Baal in Samaria and worshipped there.

Jezebel was notorious for killing any known prophets. Elijah was very disturbed and afraid. He met Obadiah, who was a devout man of the Lord. To escape Jezebel he hid about a hundred prophets in caves, in two groups of fifty each, and supplied them with food and water. Obadiah met King Ahab and told him to meet Elijah, the prophet.

Ahab on seeing him remarked, "So there you are — the worst troublemaker in Israel!"

"I'm not the troublemaker," Elijah replied, "You are — you and your father. You are disobeying the Lord's commands . . . "

He then asked the people of Israel to assemble at Mount Carmel for a contest to see which is the true God. He asked the king to send the 450 prophets of Baal and the 400 prophets of the goddess Asherah who were supporters of Queen Jezebel.

The Lord God of Elijah sent a fire down, which consumed all that was sacrificed. The false prophets of Jezebel were seized and killed by the people when their god failed.

Jezebel did not go to Mount Carmel, but King Ahab told her of the fate of her prophets. She was so angry with Elijah that she threatened to kill him within twenty-four hours. Elijah got the message and fled.

Meanwhile King Benhadad of Syria gathered his troops to fight King Ahab and Jezebel. The first attack of the Syrians failed. Then there was the second Syrian attack. Following this there was peace between Syria and Israel.

The Prophet Elisha asked one of his young prophets to go to Gilead and anoint Jehu as King of Israel. King Ahab was killed in the battle with the Syrians. His son succeeded him. When Jehu arrived in Jezreel, Jezebel called out names to him. "You assassin! Why are you here?"

Jehu ordered the palace officials to throw her out of the window. She was thrown out and fell to the ground. Jehu's horses and chariot ran over her body. "Her remains will be scattered there like dung, so that no one will be able to identify them". These were the words of the Lord as spoken through the prophet Elijah.

Jezebel was a wicked woman and an evil queen, who did many evil deeds. This is the fate that awaits those who worship Baal. Jehu ruled Samaria as king for twenty-eight years.

Think It Over:

God works in mysterious ways.

God's ways are not always our ways.

We have to try to understand God's ways.

People who work for God — priests, lady ministers and others — must reflect the nature of God in their actions. "That others may see the goodness that they do and give glory to God."

Dr G. Reth

JOANNA (Giver)

Luke 8:1-3

Jesus moved around like a nomad during His public ministry. He had no income and no definite place to stay. There were some holy women who cooked for Him and who offered hospitality. These included Martha and Mary.

The name Joanna is mentioned twice with regard to the holy women who followed Jesus and provided him with some resources. Joanna was married to Chuza, who was an officer in Herod's court. Women like her "used their own resources to help Jesus and His disciples".

She was there when Jesus was crucified. She was there when they went to see His body after the hurried burial, to apply some balm. She was an early witness to the resurrection.

Perhaps she had a disease of which she was healed. Luke mentions that "some women who had been healed of evil spirits and diseases".

It was to give back something in gratitude for their cures that these women followed Jesus. Not many people would have the courage to follow the Master, especially when there was controversy and trouble. There could be trouble for the husband as he was an officer (some scholars mention him as a manager) in King Herod's court.

Another holy woman mentioned along with her is Susanna. She too used her money and resources to help Jesus and His disciples. This name (well known from the Civil War song *Oh Susanna*) though old-fashioned is still very popular. I know of recent babies — Sue Ann and Baby Sue and Susan. Susanna means lily, a beautiful flower. Even Our Lord was fascinated by the lilies of the field.

JOBANA (Job's Wife)
Job 2:9

The Book of Job is one book that readers of the Bible prefer to avoid. There is only sorrow in it. God only knows what was the real intention of including this in the Bible. It has only given the enemies of the Bible ammunition to attack the Word of God, and the Good God. When we say it is from God all good things flow, we expect only goodies. Can the Good God deliberately allow bad things to happen to the good creatures He loves?

This brings us to the $72,000 question: "Why do bad things happen to good people?" Another $60,000 question that perplexes many is: "Why do good things happen to bad people?" You probably know of many bad people who don't deserve good things — living in luxury with goodies and flashy expensive cars and not sweating for their daily bread.

On the other hand, we have the good people who are so poor and unfortunate, who beg for their daily bread and necessities, and bad things happen to them. Sad! Sad!

Once upon a time in the sixties I worked in a slum clearance project in a very remote part of Madras, now called Chennai, in South India. People living there were so poor that they had almost nothing of value — except their lives. Even water was very scarce. We went round with some social workers begging for supplies. This organization was linked with the SCI (Service Civil Internationale), a French social service organization started by Pierre Cérésole after World War II. I helped out as a cook and looked after the dispensary. Whilst working on the project I became so ill that I was confined in the isolation ward in the Infectious Diseases Hospital in Madras. I was bleeding internally and lost consciousness. I became skin and bones and lost all my hair. By the grace of God — yes, a bargain with my Creator got me my life. I had to be taught to use my hands and taught to walk. Death was so very common in that ward — due to cholera and typhoid. Even in the slum clearance project, where I volunteered, death was a way of life. Infant mortality was high in the nearby slums. Sometimes I wondered about Job and his family — was the suffering all that necessary? Must we suffer and then only merit Heaven?

The enemies of the Christian faith and the Bible point out occasionally that the picture of God, characterized on the Old Testament and in the story of Job, is that of a sadistic God. "He must have had fun watching the unfortunate suffer. He could be in the role of a puppeteer pulling the strings and watching the reaction". These are two common observations.

The other day a lady who had insurmountable problems gave me similar comments and did not fail to include poor Job. "God must be having fun watching us suffer and then crawling on our knees to Him".

No, no, no! Our God is a suffering God. Our God came down here to impress this concept into our thick skulls, so that it could be etched in our minds. We know that Jesus was born in this world as a poor unfortunate babe, in a stable with animals and shepherds to be His onlookers. He had no riches; no house to call His home. He was like a nomad, with very little attachments. His foster father was a poor carpenter in Nazareth. He worked as a carpenter. He ate simple meals prepared by His mother, Mary. He was insulted and thrashed to glory, being whipped in public and paraded from one institution to another. He was discredited by the literary and religious people. He was publicly humiliated like a common criminal guilty of a mortal sin, yet he was sinless. He was stripped naked and crucified between two thieves. All this was done as a public execution. Yes, He suffered — when He did not have to. Yes, He had the power to save Himself from all the atrocities — but He chose to drink the bitter cup. Why?

Because He wanted to show us that bad things can happen to good people, even to the Son of God. Now we get the answer to the second question raised earlier.

Coming back to Job, the author has gone somewhat overboard. The friends of Job explain all misfortunes and suffering in traditional religious terms: "Maybe he was a sinner".

But, Job is portrayed as being too simple and honest. That's why, like stories in Greek mythology, the conclusion is good. Job is restored to his former condition with even greater prosperity than before. Also, God reprimands Job's friends for failing to decipher the meaning of Job's misery. You will notice that only poor Job sensed and had faith that God is greater than traditional religion had portrayed Him.

His wife is mentioned as one who is a fellow sufferer. "Then Satan left the Lord's presence and made sores break out all over Job's body. Job went and sat by the rubbish heap and took a piece of broken pottery to scrape his sores. His wife said to him, "You are still as faithful as ever, aren't you? Why don't you curse God and die?"

She must have been deeply disgusted at all the tragedy and misery that was troubling Job and his family. Job's children and servants were all killed (one servant escaped to come and report to him). His sheep and property were all destroyed.

In spite of everything bad that happened Job did not sin by blaming God. His reply to his dear wife was, "You are talking nonsense! When God sends us something good, we welcome it. How can we complain when he sends us trouble?"

But Job was human, very human and under pressure did finally complain to God and wished that he was never born.

"Curse that night for letting me be born, for exposing me to trouble and grief. I wish that I had died in my mother's womb or died the moment I was born".

He was only human and buckled under all sorts of stressors, but he did not curse God as incited by his wife.

Generally, women can handle pressures well but Job's wife had seen the bottom of the pit and that was enough for her. In the end she must have made her peace with God and relented. God must have forgiven her and this is evidenced by the good children she bore and the prosperity that followed.

She became the mother of seven handsome sons and three daughters. The Bible says, "There were no other women in the whole world as beautiful as Job's daughters". The oldest daughter was Jemimah, second Keziah and third Keren. Job gave each daughter an inheritance. Job lived for one hundred and forty years as a very rich man. His wife too lived happily with a long life. Moral? Good things come to them that wait.

Think It Over:

If you want rainbows in your life you must put up with the rain.

JOCHEBED (Jehovah's glory)

Exodus 2:1-2

Jochebeb was a Levite married to Amram and the mother of a famous man in the Bible — Moses. She lived in Egypt as a slave. She could not keep the infant Moses in the house, because of the Law of the Egyptians — to kill the newborn male babies. So she allowed the babe to be put in cradle made of reeds and floated in the waters of the Nile.

This cradle floated close to where the pharaoh's daughter was bathing and she found the child and named the baby Moses (out of the water).

It must have been very traumatic for the young mother to be alienated from her baby, but this was survival. The best part is how the child was reunited with the mother. She managed to nurse the baby.

Later, as Moses grew up, it must have been really difficult for this mother to be Moses's mother. There were too many stressful events in the life of Moses, especially after he was banished into the wilderness and he returned to save his people. "Let my people go," he pleaded with to the pharaoh.

Jochebeb had other children, Miriam and Aaron. Moses was special — because he was the Law Giver and the deliverer. She had a special name to highlight the glory of God — Jehovah's glory.

JULIA (Hebrew: Chaste. Roman: Female Form of Julius)
Romans 16:3-5

"Greetings also to Andronicus and Julia, fellow-Jews who were in prison with me; they are well known among the apostles, and they became Christians before I did" *(Romans 16:7).*

The name Julia is one of the most popular names in the Christian and non-Christian world. Julia Roberts is an Academy Award-winning actress. Julius Caesar was one of the greatest Roman emperors.

This young lady would have remained unknown and would have languished in jail unrecognized if not for Paul, the self-styled Apostle of Our Lord Jesus.

Julia was already a Christian and was proud of it. For being a witness and professing the Christian faith there was the penalty of being stripped of one's rights as a citizen, thrown into jail and subjected to harsh torture.

We have one life to lead in this world and we could lead it well without much suffering. There is so much to enjoy and so much to see in this wonderful world. Would you forsake it all for your faith (the faith of Jesus Christ)? Remember this took place in the 1st Century when Christianity was not yet a global success — as it is now. Today we are everywhere, and the mightiest nations are all Christian. Today Christianity is the greatest power on earth! At that time — nobody was sure it would succeed. The Romans were pagans, and Christians were a scanty minority — gathering in underground places like the catacombs.

Julia was mentioned by name in the Letter of Paul to the Romans as she was a prominent person. Perhaps there were also many unnamed sufferers in the prisons. They chose to live and die for the Lord — whom they knew only indirectly from Peter and the Apostles. Consider the faith of Julia: would we have sacrificed our lives as readily for the Lord? What sacrifices are we making to further spread the message and the Good News of the Lord?

KETURAH

Genesis 25:1-4

Abraham initially had two sons, Ishmael and Isaac (the former through Hagar, his maid, and the later through Sarah). Abraham had a concubine named Keturah who bore him six sons — Zimran, Jokshan, Medan Midian, Ishbak, and Shuah.

It was common in those days for rulers and rich men to have wives and concubines. Their children also inherited properties.

Abraham was favoured by God. He was promised many children. It was not wrong for him to have many wives and concubines. The only unfortunate episode was that of Hagar, the Egyptian handmaid of Sarah. Hers was the first instance of surrogate pregnancy in the Bible.

The story is sad because Abraham used her and then threw her away in the desert with her son to perish. If only he had led her to a safe place, or let her live in a house where he could maintain her and his son, that would have been all right. But to leave her in the desert — just because Sarah could not tolerate her or because he had another son — does not seem right.

Apparently this did not happen to Keturah and she seems to have managed well after Sarah's death.

Think It Over:

Suffering is necessary in this world to some extent. Only God can remove sufferings that come as a form of evil. Fasting is a form of penance and a form of voluntary suffering. Fasting is also a form of spiritual exercise that can win graces from God. Interestingly, women can stand the periods of fasting better than men. After all, they have more subcutaneous fat and adipose tissue than men.

LAURIMA

Luke 18:1-6

The Gospel message of Luke is unique in many ways. It is the best presentation of God as the forgiver. In this Gospel, there are many references to God's mercy and to the power of prayer.

It contains messages that are found only in Luke's Gospel, such as *The Gloria* (the angels' song), the shepherds' visit, and the parables of the Good Samaritan and the Lost Son.

Speaking of the parables of Jesus, there is only one mentioned in the Gospel, thanks to Luke, about perseverance in prayer. This is also the only parable involving a woman, and that a widow. This is not an ordinary shy woman. She is a bold woman who can give stress to a judge "who neither feared God nor respected man". "And there was a widow in that same town who kept coming to him and pleading for her rights, saying, 'Help me against my opponent!'"

Jesus said this judge refused to act on her case. He just could not be bothered. Maybe she was not important to him. After all, she was a widow, and a helpless one. She must have gone repeatedly to plead with the judge to do something for her. Her opponent was having the upper hand and she had no one except the law. In fact, in ancient English, the word Law meant the Lord. This was prayer; appealing to God, her Lord of Mercy.

The judge must have reconsidered the issues. Jesus said the judge did some 'self-talking'. This is a stress-relieving technique. The judge said to himself, 'Even though I don't fear God or respect man, yet because of all the trouble this widow is giving me, I will see to it that she gets her rights. If I don't, she will keep on coming and finally wear me out!'

I feel a sense of humour reading this passage. Visualize the scene; the learned, fearless and corrupt judge pacing up and down biting his nails in anguish. What does he decide? — Grant her the favour before she wears me out.

Now Jesus put this poser to us: if the corrupt and fearless judge could be moved, what about the All-Merciful God who is the symbol of divine love? God will grant us the favour we seek. Let it be success in an examination or a seemingly impossible task. Persist in asking and God Almighty will grant it. Never doubt the power of God. God will answer your prayer if God is impressed by your confidence in God's Omnipotent Power. Human beings are the only creatures of God that can think and pray — a dialogue of supplication, a special communication.

Think It Over:

The human mind is one frontier that is quite perplexing. There are regions in the mind where strange desires lurk.

We need to develop a healthy mind and fill it with clean, positive ideas.

Often we must be mindful of our Creator and seek ways to please Him. Prayer is a manner of reaching out to God. We must never be tired of prayer.

Dr G. Reth

The best prayer, it is said, is the paternoster. The modified form begins with "Our God who art in Heaven..." This is a non-gender form.

I can declare with conviction that in times of distress the best antidote is the Our Father. The particular sentence I find interesting and effective is, "Deliver us from all evil". Evil exists everywhere and only Almighty God can rescue us from the clutches of evil. He is our Creator. We have His guarantee card with our baptism. Use this powerful mantra. Prayer — it works!

LEAH (Hebrew: Tired)
Genesis 29:16

Jacob, the patriarch, had an interesting encounter with Laban when he went to the East looking for a wife among his kindred. He met Rachel in the fields and it was love at first sight. Jacob told Laban "I will work seven years for you, if you will let me marry Rachel".

Laban agreed to the marriage with the young and pretty Rachel. But after the seven years he was tricked on the wedding night when Laban slipped Leah, the older sister, into the honeymoon bed. Only next day did he discover to his distress who his woman was the previous night. Laban's excuse? He blamed it on the custom: "It is not the custom here to give the younger daughter in marriage before the elder." Then he was asked to make another seven years contract to work for Rachel. Jacob agreed.

The Lord saw that Leah was loved less so He made it possible for Leah to have many children. Her first born was Reuben (Hebrew: has seen my trouble). The second was Simeon and the third was Levi. The fourth was Judah (meaning praised). She gave birth to four sons in succession; then two more sons and one daughter. She was really *tired* of childbearing and that was her name.

Throughout the Bible passages we learn that Leah was loved less and Rachel more. Yet it is difficult to comprehend the mind of the writer. Jacob slept with Leah and had sex with her and that is how he got his children. She just happened to be more fertile, thanks to God. When Rachel died she was buried in the wilderness. Leah was buried in the special tomb assigned by Jacob, and later Jacob was laid to rest next to her.

Leah was one sourpuss — every time she had a child she gave a name to signify her thoughts.

1 — Surely my husband will love me now *(Genesis 29:32)*.

2 — Because the Lord heard that I am not loved, he gave me this one too *(Genesis 29:32)*.

3 — Now at last my husband will be bound more tightly to me because I have borne him three sons *(Genesis 29:34)*.

4 — This time I will praise the Lord *(Genesis 29:35)*.

It was Judah, whose lineage featured in the South Kingdom and in one of the titles of Jesus Christ — Lion from Judah's tribe *(Revelation 5:5)*. Rachel, the unfortunate girl who was beautiful and shapely was barren for a while. She became desperate. She said to Jacob, "Give me children, or I will die".

This made Jacob angry and he said to Rachel, "I can't take the place of God. He is the one who keeps you from having children".

Then Rachel tried surrogate pregnancy by offering her slave Bilhah — the womb-for-rent technique. "In this way I can become a mother through her". Rachel named Bilhah's son Dan. Her second son was Naphtali (meaning fight).

Now the competition became more of a fight. Leah gave her slave, Zilpah, to Jacob. This son was Gad (meaning luck). Then Leah was very happy the technique worked — especially with the next son of Zilpah, whom she named Happy, or Asher.

Then came the mandrake incident involving Leah and Rachel. Leah said to Jacob, "You are going to sleep with me tonight, because I have paid for you with my son's mandrakes". The son who resulted from that encounter was Issachar (meaning reward). Leah became pregnant again with a sixth son whom she named Zebulun (gift accepted) Leah's next child was a daughter named Dinah.

Rachel had one more child and her last son was Joseph, whom Jacob loved very much. After this child Jacob decided to leave Laban with his family and flock. Leah cannot be called unlucky, by any account. She had a competitive sister but in those days it was all in the family; you just had to take it easy and not be tired mentally.

LETICIA (Lot's Daughter)
Genesis 19:30-38

There is, in the Book of Leviticus (18:1-30), a definite order from God about forbidden sexual practices. This was given to Moses. In it is contained rules and regulations about sexual intercourse. Homosexuality is forbidden and also sexual relations with animals.

In spite of all these commandments Lot's daughters had sex with their father and begot children. They did it in turns every night. Why did they do it? What was wrong with these young girls? They were supposed to be from a very holy and exemplary family.

Haran was the father of Lot. Terah was the father of Abraham, Nahor and Haran. Haran died in his hometown of Ur, in Babylonia (today's Iraq). Abraham, who was known earlier as Abram, was seventy-five years old when he moved out from Haran (the city) as the Lord had told him to, with his wife and his nephew Lot, and went to Canaan.

While they were in southern Canaan there were frequent quarrels between Abram and Lot over property and sheep, so they separated. Abram moved to Hebron. Once, when Lot was captured, Abram went to war and rescued him.

When Lot was staying close to Sodom two angels came one evening. They stayed with Lot that night. But the men of Sodom surrounded his house. They called out to Lot, "Where are the men who came to stay with you tonight? Bring them out to us". The men of Sodom wanted to have sex with them.

Lot said to them, "Friends, I beg you, don't do such a wicked thing! Look, I have two daughters who are still virgins. Let me bring them out to you, and you can do whatever you want with them. But don't do anything to these men".

The men outside became very unruly and wanted to break the door to get in: "Who are you to tell us what to do? Get out of our way, you foreigner!" The two men from inside heard the commotion and pulled Lot back into the house. Then they struck all those wicked men with blindness, so they went here and there in confusion.

Then the two angelic men told Lot to leave Sodom with his family and not to look back, because the Lord was planning to destroy Sodom and Gomorrah. Lot took his wife and two daughters and left. Then the Lord destroyed the twin cities. Lot's wife disobeyed. She was too curious (that was a flaw) and was changed into a pillar of salt when she looked back. Lot went to Zoar but was afraid to stay there so they moved to the hills and rested in a cave. The father was tired and rested. The older sister told the other sister, "Our father is getting old, and there are no men in the whole world to marry us so that we can have children. Come on, let's make our father drunk, so that we can sleep with him and have children by him". So they gave him wine to drink and then had intercourse with him.

The older sister had a son this way and named him Moab (meaning from my father). The younger sister had a son and she named him Benammi (meaning son of my relative). This is how the Moabites and Ammonites (Benammi) originated.

The Menorah:

The many-branched Menorah, used on Chanukkah, is modelled on the seven-branched one. One day's supply of oil lasted for eight days.

Menorah, the seven branch candelabrum used in the Temple of Jerusalem. *(Exodus 25:31-40).*

LOIS
2 Timothy 1:5

Lois was the grandmother of Timothy. Paul's second Letter to Timothy contains his advice on the dangers of becoming involved in foolish and ignorant arguments, which do no good, but which ruin those who listen to them.

In the second letter he also mentions the faith of Lois (the grandmother), and Timothy's mother, Eunice, who was a Jewish Christian. Timothy's father was Greek.

By this declaration we know that Timothy comes from a good family background. There are three generations; all are rich in faith. Paul's Letter is also a sad one. In it he says, "You know that everyone in the province of Asia, including Phygelus and Hermogenes, has deserted me". This Letter was written from his prison cell. "I suffer and I am even chained like a criminal. But the Word of God is not in chains..."

It was good people like Lois who kept the faith going. We need the young and the old to propagate the Good News of the Lord. Grandmothers all over the world, please join in the crusade.

Paul was lucky to have friends like Lois and Eunice. These ladies were new converts to Christianity. They took risks to accommodate Paul and meet his needs. Paul was a charismatic motivator and was able to enlist many strangers to the fold of Christianity. What was Paul's great gift?

LOTISUMA (Lot's Wife)
Genesis 19:1-26

Lot's wife may not have been a bad woman, to be punished in such dramatic manner. How was she punished? She was turned into a pillar of salt.

The two angels sent by God to punish the people of Sodom and Gomorrah were met by Abraham. He prepared a meal for them and soon learned that they were set on destroying the entire twin cities. Abraham pleaded with them to spare Lot and his family as they were related to him (Lot was his nephew). The angels said if there were ten people in the two cities who were good they would not destroy the cities. But there were not, so they had to destroy everything there.

The two angels went to Sodom in the evening and saw Lot sitting at the gate of the city. He invited them in to spend the night with him and his family. "No, we will spend the night here in the city square". However, Lot managed to convince them to put up for the night with his family. But it was a horrible night; there were too many disturbances. Imagine the local sex perverts coming to Lot's house and asking for the angelic men to be turned to them for sex. This prompted Lot to make a shocking offer to them in order to save the two men from harassment. He offered his two daughters who were still virgins and who had never had intercourse with any man before.

Anyway, Lot and his wife were lucky as these two angels had extraordinary powers. They shut the door and struck all the men outside with blindness so they could not find the door.

Then they asked Lot to assemble all his family members and relatives and get them out at once. What did Lot do? He ran to get the men to whom his daughters were engaged to be married and told them the bad news of destruction. They laughed and thought he was joking. Time was running out for the twin cities. So the two men took Lot, his wife and his daughters by the hand and led them out of the city. One of the angels advised them, "Run for your lives! Don't look back and don't stop in the valley. Run to the hills, so that you won't be killed".

Lot bargained with the angels to allow them to reach halfway and still be spared. He got his request and so they reached Zoar safely. "But Lot's wife looked back and was turned into a pillar of salt".

Perhaps she was a vain woman. There were many ideas of regret in her mind that caused her to look back. Probably she had to leave behind many precious items in her home. It is difficult to just get up and run out with what you have on your body. But that was the command.

She must have been a very curious woman. It is even said, "curiosity killed the cat". In this case there was also an element of disobedience to an angelic command. Even our Lord quoted this incident and mentioned, "Remember Lot's wife!"

Today in the same region there are salt pillars that stand out like stalagmites. One particular pillar there looks like a petrified woman and is referred to as Mrs Lot by the tourist guides. I prefer to call her Lotisuma. The heat is unbearable, often averaging 138°F. The region is considered the lowest point on earth (400 metres below sea level). No bird flies over the area and it is considered unhealthy — by all creatures as well as local folk.

Think It Over:

Give to God what is God's and to fellow human beings what belongs to them. Keeo your promises to God.

LYDIA (Hebrew: Work)

Acts 16:14

She lived in Greece in the city of Philippi. She was a good friend of Paul — the Apostle. She was originally from Thyatira, a city in Asia, famous for purple dye and purple clothes. Those days purple was linked with royalty and she had a thriving business.

"One of those who heard us was Lydia from Thyatira, who was a dealer in purple cloth. She was a woman who worshipped God, and the Lord opened her mind to pay attention to what Paul was saying. After she and the people of her house had been baptized, she invited Paul: "Come and stay in my house if you have decided that I am a true believer in the Lord".

She was a rich good woman who was very charitable to the early Christian community. Not all rich women are good or charitable. They may show off to get publicity and more honours. But Lydia was different because she was a true believer, who "worshipped God".

On another occasion Paul and Silas were dragged through the streets, their clothes were torn and they were whipped in public and put in prison *(Acts 16, 19-24)*. On their release, following an earthquake, they went to Lydia's house to rest. There they met the believers and spoke words of encouragement to them.

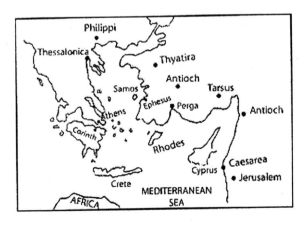

103

MARTHA (Hebrew: Rebellious)
Luke 10:38-42; John 11:5-27

In Bethany, a few miles out of Jerusalem, lived a very loving family of three members: Martha, Mary and Lazarus. En route to Galilee or Jerusalem this is a good place to rest, far from the hustle and bustle of the city life. It was one of Jesus' favourite houses to rest in and even preach in.

Even on a recent visit to this house — I was able to understand that the setting was ideal for Jesus. The tomb of Lazarus is also there and one needs to go down about twenty-seven steps to reach it. I managed to squeeze myself in to lie down on the icy-cold rock tomb where Our Lord performed the resurrection miracle for Lazarus. Judging by the size of the house and compound they must have been rich people.

The Gospel reading for the passage on Martha and Mary *(Luke 10: 38-42)*, where her name is mentioned first, is an interesting one for preachers. Sadly, Martha is always given poor marks. She is even made to look like she was rebuked by Our Lord Jesus. Was Martha her real name? Yes — Rebellious.

In the Gospel passages she is mentioned first, then Mary. If you analyse the passages well you will discover that Mary was the docile one who sat at the feet of Jesus to listen to His parables and explanations. Somebody had to be busy with the household chores. What about the cooking and serving of the food? What about housekeeping? Jesus never went anywhere alone; He always had a group with him. Men eat a lot. These were grown men — Apostles and disciples. Probably there were some holy women too. Martha had to be bothered with all those details. It is only natural; perhaps it is a maternal instinct.

Jesus came to a village where a woman named Martha welcomed him into her home. She had a sister named Mary, who sat at the feet of the Lord and listened to His teachings. Martha was upset over all the work she had to do, so she came and said, "Lord, don't you care that my sister has left me to do all the work by myself?

Tell her to come and help me!" And Jesus is supposed to have told Martha not to worry and let Mary do just what she was doing. It is kind of difficult not to complain when faced with a lot of household chores. Anyway, Martha took the rebuke in the right spirit. She, after all, complained to the Lord. She had confidence in Him.

It was, after all, the same Martha who in the Gospel of John (11:20-22) uttered, "If You had been here, Lord, my brother would not have died! But I know that even now God will give You whatever You ask Him for".

Then Jesus told her that he will come to life. "I know that he will rise to life on the last day," she declared.

Jesus told Martha, "I am the resurrection and the life". These were very powerful words. He had never been more direct about His supernatural self. "Whoever believes in Me will live, even though he dies; and whoever lives and believes in Me will never die. Do you [Martha] believe this?"

Martha replied, "Yes, Lord! I do believe that You are the Messiah, the Son of God, who was to come into the world". What a declaration of faith in public. There was a funeral and a mourning crowd. Jesus was with His entourage.

After Martha said this, she went back and called her sister Mary privately. "The Teacher is here," she told her, "and is asking for you". Overcome with emotion and grief Mary was inside crying. After all, it was mentioned "many Judeans had come to see Martha and Mary to comfort them . . . " But it was Martha who ran out to meet Jesus when she heard Jesus was coming. Mary stayed in the house where her friends were comforting her. She got up and ran out and the people "thought she was going to the grave to weep there".

Mary spoke to Jesus saying, "If You had been here, my brother would not have died". Jesus saw them all weeping and Jesus wept openly. "His heart was touched, and He was deeply moved". When Jesus wept, the people said, "See how much He loved him!" Jesus was very human. He too knew suffering and stress. He came here to be part of the whole human drama of life. Deeply moved, Jesus went to the tomb. "Take the stone away!" Jesus ordered.

Martha spoke again (she was bold), "There will be a bad smell, Lord. He has been buried four days!" Jesus spoke to reinforce their faith and then came His order to the dead man: "Lazarus, come out!" The dead man came out with his hands and feet bound with cloth. This was the resurrection of Lazarus from the dead.

The next visit that Jesus made to Bethany was six days before His death (and the Passover). Martha, as usual, prepared dinner and served Him. Lazarus was one of those sitting at the table with Jesus.

Mary, her sister, then did the anointing of Jesus with a very expensive perfume. She poured it on Jesus' feet and wiped them with her hair.

Judas Ischariot asked, "Why wasn't this perfume sold for 300 silver coins and the money given to the poor?"

But Jesus rebuked him, "Leave her alone!" He mentioned that what she was doing was the anointing "for the day of my burial". Many of them did not know that Jesus was close to His death.

Bethany, the home of Martha and Mary and Lazarus, became very famous because of the resurrection miracle. There was even a plot to kill Lazarus because of this miracle *(John 12:9-11)*.

Reflect On This:

For God loved the world so much that He gave His only Son, so that everyone who believes in Him may not die but have eternal life *(John 3:16)*.

MARY MOTHER OF JESUS (Hebrew: Bitter)
Matthew 1:18-24, Luke 2:1-7

This special person needs no introduction. She is the most famous woman in the Bible. In fact, I can safely declare that she is the most popular woman in history and presently in the world. Proof?

1 — There are shrines and churches dedicated to her — more than to any other woman.

2 — She has the greatest number of names linked to her — Mirim, Marian, Mariology, Mario, Mariotte, and other names in combination.

3 — There are cities and states dedicated to her — Maryland, Maryville, St Mary's Town, etc.

4 — Pilgrimage shrines attract thousands of devotees in all the continents. In France there is Lourdes; in Ireland there is Knock; in Mexico there is Our Lady of Guadalupe; in Italy there is Our Lady of Loreto; in Portugal Our Lady of Fatima; in India there is Velankanni; in USA Washington National Shrine of the Virgin; in Turkey there is the Meryem Ana Evi, (House of the Virgin) on Mount Mary in Ephesus.

Important events in the life of Mary as associated with Jesus:

1 — Her marriage to Joseph, the carpenter.

2 — The Annunciation. The Angel Gabriel appeared to her and told her that she had found favour with God. "Hail Mary, full of grace, The Lord is with you. Blessed are you among women . . ." This was in Nazareth.

3 — The meeting with Elizabeth at Ain Karim and her famous utterances in the Magnificat.

4 — Her journey to Bethlehem to register for the census with Joseph.

5 — The birth of Jesus in Bethlehem in a stable.

6 — The presentation in the Temple of Jerusalem.

7 — The flight to Egypt to escape Herod.

8 — The family settled down in Nazareth.

9 — The twelve-year-old Jesus was lost in Jerusalem and He questions the elders.

10 — Miracle at Cana: "Do whatever He tells you".

11 — The public ministry of Jesus — following Jesus to most of the places of preaching.

12 — The trial of Jesus and the Crucifixion. Mary stood by the Cross.

13 — The Pentecostal happening. Mary was there with the Apostles praying. She was their guiding and unifying force.

Her virtues keep the Church going in many lands where women are honoured. There have been several apparitions of Mary.

Let me end with a note to those who hate Mary, and burn her pictures or rosaries or destroy any objects concerning her. Even her statues are broken or defaced. I have repaired statues of the Blessed Mother even in Los Angeles and offered to repair the famous bronze defaced statue in Ephesus — the last known home of Mary. They did not accept the offer as the custodians feel that the defaced statue with the details should exist so to show the attitude of a section of mankind. (My services by the way are free of any charges.)

After all, let's reason it out — she is the symbol of a good woman with all saintly virtues. She harmed no one during her lifetime; nor did she say any harsh or sinful word. She cannot be linked to any evil, in the past, present or in the future. The bad part of the deal is that a good number of women are there ready to raise their fists at the mother of Christ — saying she is a stumbling block and that Marian devotions amount to pagan worship or idol worship. These women should come to their senses. She is a woman and a symbol of the woman who needs recognition and some honour. We must have some charity and decency in our hearts. We should love her as we would — just as we know her to be — some saintly mother. Praising or honouring her is something God would encourage. This is not the same as in some religions where there is the worship of a female goddess. Mary is not a goddess. She was a saintly creature — a good wife and a good mother. Remember her as the good mother. Remember her as the good wife of Joseph and the excellent mother of Jesus Christ — your boss and mine — your Creator and mine. I'm sure there are times you gave a hamper or gift to your boss's mother to win favours with the son. Stop kidding, you don't believe in this approach.

Think It Over:

In my stress-management lectures I do mention that Mary had a very tough option. She was put under tremendous stress. It was a difficult role. She managed her stress very well. She did not buckle under and doubt God, or utter profanities. True to her name, she underwent bitter experiences but her fruit was sweet.

A FEW HIGHLIGHTS ON MARY

Firstly, she was a teenage mother. Secondly, she must have been very special to be selected from all humanity to be the spiritual vessel to bring the final Messiah into the world (all who came before him were prophets and patriarchs). He stands out, different and beyond compare. She stands different from other women — before and after).

She had a lot of patience to stand and witness silently the humiliation, torture, rejection and public execution of her only son. (I know a lot of mothers who are very vocal and wild when they are pushed to extremes by circumstances. She never lost her cool because she understood that it was a sacrifice — of a new and final covenant.)

Nobody could tell Jesus what to do or what not to do. He had His mind set. He came with a mission — to restore confidence in God. Mankind had grown weary of a punishing and revengeful God asking for bloody animal sacrifices. Yet, it was His mother, who, because of her womanly, maternal instincts, sensed the embarrassment of the newly married couple when early during the reception they had run out of drinks — wine. In those days the main drink was wine, not soft drinks or tea or coffee.

Mary spoke to Jesus asking Him to perform a miracle. She knew His potential. She must have seen the power of God in Him on a few occasions, unknown to all the others. Jesus, of course, refused at first saying that it was not His time yet. He was not ready. But His mother had her way. "Do whatever He tells you," were her words to the master of the house and attendants. Poor Jesus had no choice. He obeyed His mother. As a result of this He performed the first miracle in His life in a public place — to please His mother. He was not anxious to do this at that time — to begin His public ministry. But the lady had her way.

This is why many Christians believe in Mary as an interceder. She can put in a word for you because of her very close links with the Divine Master.

MARY CLOPAS
John 19:25-37

There were three Marys at the crucifixion scene: Mary, the mother of Jesus; His mother's sister Mary Clopas, and Mary of Magdala.

Jesus saw His mother and the disciple He loved standing there; so He said to His mother, "He is your son". Then He said to the disciple, "She is your mother". From that time the disciple took her to live in his house.

Jesus did not have any brothers or sisters. Some enemies of Jesus and the Church claim that Mary, His mother, had other children. Then there are other made-up stories that Joseph, His foster-father, had other children, probably with another woman. He certainly was no widower. The mind of God would not be such as to entertain such relationships and then make the path of salvation so uncomfortable for Jesus and even His family.

God does not like to make complications like Hollywood movies. This is a holy story and God in His wisdom would not make it more fanciful with various types of acquired family members.

Anyway, if there were other children, John the Evangelist would not be summoned from the cross with the dying breath of Jesus to be entrusted with the care of Jesus' mother. His mother is also told to accept John as her son. She had nowhere else to go. As for Mary Clopas, she may not be her blood sister, but is probably a relative. It stretches one's imagination to consider the wisdom of one pair of parents deciding to name two sisters with the same name. There is no shortage of names, and the name Mary, though popular now (made so by Jesus' mother), meant nothing sweet, only bitterness. (Marah in Hebrew means bitter.)

MARY, SISTER OF LAZARUS
Luke 10:38-41

Martha welcomed Jesus into the house. She had a sister named Mary, who sat at the feet of Our Lord and listened to His teaching. She was the quieter one of the two sisters. She symbolized the good listener — the academic-minded student. Our Lord complimented her on her choice — to be the one who would honour the presence of a holy person of God by giving the attention He deserves. It is not often we have a person of the stature of Jesus coming to our house. You need to stop whatever you are doing and give your undivided attention.

Jesus told Martha, "Mary has chosen the right thing, and it will not be taken away from her". Mary chose to sit and listen to God's words. We must have our priorities. God must always come first only then the other cares. If God calls you to serve Him you must leave everything behind and attend to Him. We must respect God, our Creator, and heed Him.

Mary, the sister of Lazarus, is also the woman who poured expensive perfume on Jesus and anointed Him. She poured this on the feet of Jesus and wiped it with her long tresses. The Apostles saw this and did not approve of this wastage. Jesus had to quip in and say, "Leave her alone! Let her keep what she has for the day of my burial" *(John 12:7)*.

It is quoted in Mark 14, "Some of the people there became angry and said to one another, 'What was the use of wasting the perfume? It could have been sold for more than three hundred silver coins and the money given to the poor!'" Thus they criticized her harshly.

Jesus praised His Mother, "Now, I assure you that wherever the gospel is preached all over the world, what she has done will be told in memory of her" *(Mark 14:9)*.

The story involving Martha and Mary teaches us about women. They are different from one another. Some are interested in attending to the affairs of the home whilst others exist only to seek God. (Blessed are the nuns and holy women. They have left everything to serve God.)

MARY MAGDALENE (Tower)

Mark 16:9

This is the other Mary in the Bible that people gossip about in riddles. She is variously referred to as a woman possessed by seven demons *(Mark 16:9)* or as a great sinner. She is even spoken of as being an adulteress or a prostitute. People can get carried away by words. One famous doctor in giving me tips on how to be successful as a private medical practitioner told me, "The whole business is a form of prostitution. We have to please people." So please be kind in the selection of words — lest they stereotype successful doctors as prostitutes.

This Mary was originally from Magdala (this is a city on the Sea of Galilee between Capernaum and Tiberias — where Jesus spent a lot of time preaching. The signboard is still there pointing the direction to Magdala (which means tower). It is believed there was a large tower on the seafront similar to a lighthouse.

Mary was very beautiful and was much desired by many for her dancing talents. She danced as if she was possessed with some abnormal energy and was thought to be harbouring demons — seven to be exact! All this is a matter of interpretation by the beholder. Even these days we have wild dancers who are exploited for their beauty and skills.

Anyway she must have been good in reality because she recognized the goodness of the Master. She changed, and changed to such an extent that she became the disciple who hugged the cross and cried. She was also at the tomb and was the first person to see the Risen Christ. That's a special honour. She spoke to Him and then went on to spread the good news. She became the tower (Magdala).

I just cannot help singing and playing the Lloyd Webber song, *I Don't Know How To Love Him*. It's an excellent piece of music set with well-chosen lyrics. Mary of Magdala really loved our Lord as the Messiah.

Jesus appeared to Mary *(Mark 16:9)* and gave her instructions. She touched Him, as she first mistook Him for the gardener. Then she heard His tone; He called her by name. She exclaimed, "Rabboni" (Teacher). Mary knew Our Lord well and realized He was Christ the Resurrected Lord *(John 20:16-18)*. Even the Apostles and disciples were surprised to know that Mary spoke, touched and received instructions from Jesus. God loves sinners — especially repentant ones. Mary represents us — sinners. Jesus loves us. Christian tradition has it that after the death of Our Lord Mary of Magdala went to live with Mary, the mother of Jesus, as her maid. She travelled with her to Ephesus as the second Holy Family with John the Evangelist. She died and is buried at Mount Mary in Ephesus, Turkey. There is a shrine there. I went to this shrine.

When I had a choice of where to send my eldest son to school, I chose St Mary Magadalen School in adjacent Beverly Hills, Los Angeles. We have always loved this wonderful character who represents us all — repentant sinners. There is also a church within the Church of the Holy Sepulchre in Jerusalem dedicated to her, at the scene of the apparition of the Risen Lord.

Quotable Quotes:

Most of all the glitter that we are attracted to started as items that lacked lustre. *Savez-vous?* Coal and diamond.

Dr G. Reth

A journey of a thousand miles must begin with a single step.

Chinese proverb

It is better to light a candle than to curse the darkness.

Anon

Lots of people can initiate a good activity but it is only the hero who endures and keeps it going.

Dr G. Reth

Mary, with her traditions in the Church is not a stumbling block but a mother who attracts many of her earthly children to know her divine Son.

Dr G. Reth

MERAB (Hebrew: Unlucky)
1 Samuel 18:17-19

Then Saul said to David "Here, here is my elder daughter Merab. I will give her to you as your wife on condition that you serve me as a brave and loyal soldier . . . " David was happy. He said he was unworthy of such a great honour — and agreed gladly. But, when the time came for Merab to be given to David, she was given to Adriel from Meholah.

Saul, the first King of Israel, was a bad character. He used his daughters to tantalize David. In reality he was hoping to honour David and have him killed in battle. The honour was to give him an important assignment. One such assignment was to kill one hundred Philistines and bring their foreskins to Saul. "All the king wants from you as payment for the bride is the foreskins of a hundred dead Philistines . . . " *(1 Samuel 18:24-27).*

David and his men went out and killed two hundred Philistines "and counted them all out to him". What a victorious presentation! They died for nothing.

Saul once tried to kill David by throwing three spears at him while the talented lad was playing his harp. Saul also tried to kill Jonathan, his own son, for befriending David. "Saul threw his spear at Jonathan to kill him . . . " *(1 Samuel 20:33-34).*

Merab was unlucky; she had a bad father who would have destroyed her marriage. Some in-laws do interfere excessively in the lives of the young people and strain relationships.

She married Adriel, son of Barzillai and had five sons. David handed over these sons to the people of Gibeon, who hanged them on the mountain. Why? The answers are in 2 Samuel 21:1-7.

MICHAL (Hebrew: Who is like God)
1 Samuel 14:49

Michal was the daughter of Saul. The name Michal is the same as that of the Archangel, meaning Who is like God. But this lady, the first wife of David, was an unfortunate one. Unlike the other wives of David she was childless. It must have caused her great sorrow — for in Hebrew culture to be barren would be interpreted as being cursed by God.

She was also unfortunate in that she had a bad father, who got her married to David with ulterior motives. Firstly, he wanted to show that he had high esteem for the young warrior and considered him fit to be his son-in-law. Secondly, and for a more important reason he wanted to put him in an uncomfortable position with the Philistines. In one of the encounters he hoped David would be killed.

For a start he demanded that David bring one hundred foreskins of the Philistines, before he could marry his daughter, Michal. David instead brought two hundred of these and "counted them all out to him, so that he might become his son-in-law". Michal in reality, loved David very much and Saul knew that too. Saul told his son Jonathan that he planned to kill David because he was very popular. This son, who was a good friend of David, told David about his father's intentions.

Once Saul tried to spear David but missed. So Michal warned him about future attempts by assassins and let him escape through a window. She took a household idol and put a pillow with goats'-hair on it to resemble a man in bed. The assassins came and they were fooled. The father then confronted the daughter and chided her. She said, "He said he would kill me if I didn't help him to escape".

Saul then got Michal married to another man — Palti, son of Laish from Gallim. David, after Saul's death returned and claimed his wife Michal from Palti. Once David established his control in Jerusalem, he brought the Ark of the Covenant to the city. He ordered a great celebration and danced before everyone.

The King of Israel made a big name for himself today! He exposed

116

himself like a fool in the sight of the servant-girls of his officials! *(2 Samuel 6: 20).*

It was a rocky marriage for Michal, especially with the great sexual appetite of David. He married several wives and had many children. Michal did not have any children.

King David's Children:

David had several wives. These were the six children born while he was in Hebron for seven and a half years:

1 — Amnon — his mother was Ahinoam, from Jezreel.

2 — Daniel — his mother was Abigail, from Carmel.

3 — Absalom — his mother Maacah, daughter of King Talmai of Geshur.

4 — Adonijah — his mother was Haggith.

5 — Shephatiah — his mother was Abital.

6 — Ithream — his mother was Eglah.

While he was in Jerusalem for thirty-three years many sons were born to him:

Bathsheba gave him four sons — Shammua, Shobab, Nathan and the famous, Solomon.

He had nine other sons: Ibhar, Elishua, Elpelet, Nogah, Nepheg, Japhia, Elishama, Eliada and Eliphelet. There were other sons by his concubines, but only one daughter is listed and that was Tamar. It is strange how there were fewer daughters.

Sad Thought:

King David brought unity to Israel's warring factions. He brought about peace. But he had his own house in disorder. Was he a good father?

MIRIAM (Same as Mary: Bitterness)
Micah 6:4

She was the elder sister of Moses, the Law Giver. She acted on instructions and put Moses in a papyrus reed basket covered with tar to make it waterproof. The smart girl was nearby to fetch the real mother of the baby to nurse it for the pharaoh's daughter. She made it to the Promised Land.

The prophet Micah (a contemporary of Isaiah), lived in the southern kingdom of Judah. He said, "I rescued you from slavery; I sent Moses, Aaron, and Miriam to lead you" *(Micah 6:4).*

She thus has a special standing with her famous brothers in early Israeli history. Her name is a reflection of the bitter times when she was born as a slave in Egypt. Yet, like Mary of Magadala, she was a sweet and loving person.

Miriam, however, was once chastised by the Lord for her disapproval of Moses (see page 180). This was concerning the foreign wife of Moses — Zipporah, her sister-in-law. Women are women and they have their petty differences, whether they are prophetesses or educated professionals.

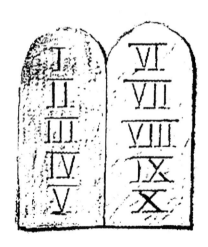

NAIMA (Naim's Wife)
Luke 7:11-17

Widows are special to God. God loves them and is merciful to them. We need in our lives funds and means to help them. During wars the worst casualty is that of the widows. How do I know? My own mother was a widow with three children when my father was gunned down. One was three years old, the next (that was me) one and a half years old and the youngest was only nineteen days old. My mother was twenty-one and jobless. The gunmen looted all that was there during the war.

The widow of Naim — Naima — was also unfortunate; her only son had died. Jesus was moved when He saw the mourners.

"The dead man was the only son of a woman who was a widow, and a large crowd from the town was with her. When the Lord saw her, His heart was filled with pity for her, and He said to her, 'Don't cry.' Then he walked over and touched the coffin . . . " He said to the dead man: "Young man! Get up, I tell you!" The dead man got up on hearing the voice of Jesus. Jesus gave the man back to his mother. The people were filled with fear and began to praise God. They shouted, "A great prophet has appeared among us!" They spread the news of this miracle to the surrounding territories. You can imagine how the smile returned to the face of the poor widow.

There are other widows highlighted in the Bible. What about Naomi, Abigail, Ruth, Anna (the prophetess), Tamar, and the widow who put the widow's mite (who was praised by Jesus)? Also, very much before Jesus was born, in the time of the prophet Elijah, there was a very poor widow from Zarephath near Sidon. It was God that instructed Elijah to go to this humble home when she was baking her last morsel of bread. She had nothing else to eat, yet God tested the faith of this Gentile woman with this prophet.

The Lord told Elijah, "Now go to the town of Zarephath, near Sidon, and stay there. I have commanded a widow who lives there to feed you" *(1 Kings 17:8-20)*. The woman knew that it was their last meal. After that they (she and her only son) would starve to death, yet she gave it to the prophet.

For her faith, during the famine there was enough food for her and her only son to last more than three years. Sometime later the young boy died. Elijah carried the boy in his arms and prayed aloud to the Lord, "O Lord my God, why have you done such a terrible thing to this widow? She has been kind enough to take care of me, and now you kill her son!" He pleaded, "O Lord my God, restore this child to life!" God in His mercy restored his life.

The widow joyfully exclaimed, "Now I know that you are a man of God and that the Lord really speaks through you!"

Even Paul has written about the qualities of a good widow *(1 Timothy 5:16)*. He mentions about widows above sixty and those who are young widows. "For some widows have already turned away to follow Satan".

In Hebrew culture widows were a despised lot. They were shunned by society. Ruth, the Moabite, and Abigail were perhaps the most fortunate ones — because they were remarried to fortunate men.

Cherubims in the Temple of Jerusalem, made out of olive wood, standing fifteen feet tall and overlaid with pure gold.

NAOMI (My Delight, My Happiness)

Ruth 1:6-13

She was a Hebrew girl but, when there was a bad famine in Israel, her husband took her and her two sons and went to live in Moab, a foreign land with foreign gods. Her husband was Elimelech, who belonged to the clan of Ephrath and was from Bethlehem. Her two sons were Mahlon and Chilion.

While they were living there the husband died. Then Naomi's two sons married two non-Israeli girls (Moabites), Orpah and Ruth. Ten years later both the sons died without any children. Now Naomi felt very depressed. The delight in her life was gone. First it was the family, second it was moving out to a strange land with strange gods to whom human sacrifice was offered. Then it was the death of her husband. Following this tragedy, it was the disappointment of acquiring two non-Israeli daughters-in-law. Both were Moabites. Then the bitter pill — the death of her two sons. She just could not take it anymore. The only silver lining in the dark clouds for the widow with two young widows was the news that God had blessed her old place of residence in Israel. There was no more famine but plenty of grain. So she decided to return.

They started out together — the three widows — back to Judah, and on the way Naomi got a brainwave and told the girls, "Go back home and stay with your mothers. May the Lord be as good to you as you have been to me and to those who have died". She kissed them goodbye. But the girls were attached to her. She was their mother-in-law. They begged and cried their hearts out to stay.

Clearly it was the voice of a very depressed woman. Her utterances clearly show how silly her arguments were. "Do you think I could have sons again for you to marry? Go back home, for I am too old to get married again". She felt the Lord had punished her. "The Lord has turned against me, and I feel very sorry for you". The girls cried and begged but it was of no use.

So Orpah (her name means gazelle — a graceful animal with beady eyes) took the cue, collected her belongings and returned.

What a shame! She was so close to becoming a believer in the true God. She wanted so much to come over to the other side. She had forsaken her people and her gods and had come to the believers' side. Now she was halfway to Judah, and asked to go back. Imagine her fate when she returned to "her people" as a widow, kicked back by her mother-in-law.

However, when she tried to encourage Ruth to return this girl refused. "Ruth, your sister-in-law has gone back to her people and to her god. Go back home with her".

Ruth was desperate, "Don't ask me to leave you! Let me go with you. Wherever you go, I will go; wherever you live, I will live. Your people will be my people, and your God shall be my God. Wherever you die, I will die, and that is where I will be buried. May the Lord's worst punishment come upon me if I let anything but death separate me from you!" She held on to Naomi's feet and begged her. When Naomi noticed how determined this girl was she said nothing more. They continued on to Bethlehem.

When she reached there the townsfolk were happy to see her. She was depressed and said, "Don't call me Naomi, call me Marah [meaning bitter, unfortunate], because Almighty God has made my life bitter. . . . the Lord Almighty has condemned me and sent me trouble".

Naomi had a rich relative named Boaz, who belonged to her husband's family. Ruth told her mother-in-law that she wanted to work for a living. "Let me go to the fields to gather the corn that the harvest workers leave. I am sure to find someone who will let me work with him". Naomi agreed.

Ruth began working in the fields gathering the leftover wheat grain, thanks to the kindness of a good man. One day while she was resting under a tree, tired, Boaz came by. "Who is that young woman?" he asked the man in charge.

"She is the foreign girl who came back from Moab with Naomi. . . . She has been working since early morning and has just now stopped to rest for a while under the shelter".

Boaz was kind to her and allowed her to work in his fields. Later he held council with the elders to settle the sale of Naomi's husband's property. But he put a condition clause that whoever buys the property should also buy Ruth, the Moabite widow. Since nobody was willing to buy the property because of this condition clause, Boaz decided to buy the property and so get Ruth.

Boaz married this girl and she was blessed with a child. The people went to congratulate Naomi. "Praise the Lord! He has given you a grandson today to take care of you. May the boy become famous in Israel! Your daughter-in-law loves you, and has done more for you than seven sons. And now she has given you a grandson, who will bring new life to you and give you security in your old age".

The townspeople were happy for Naomi because now her smiles returned. She was living up to her name (Happiness). They told everyone, "A son has been born to Naomi!" This infant later on was to become famous indeed in Israel's history. He was to be the grandfather of King David. His name was Obed. His son was Jesse.

Ruth was a Moabite, a foreigner, but unlike her fellow sister-in-law, Orpah, she was a determined young lady. She had married Naomi's son and, even after ten years of marriage, she had no children. Her husband died and she had to choose between going back to her people or following Naomi. She made the right choice.

Even when she went back to Israel with her mother-in-law, they had nothing valuable with them. Ruth had no job, yet she chose to be a determined worker to pick up some leftover grain from the fields. Her courage and personality won her a rich husband — Boaz.

Today she is remembered in history as the ancestor of King David and features in the lineage of Jesus Christ.

NIFERITA (Pharaoh's Daughter)
Exodus 2:1-10, Hebrews 11:23

Niferita was a member of the enemy but ironically she became the mother of the man who would become the Deliverer, a messiah who would deliver the Jews from slavery. There seemed to be no escape. The Jews were forced into labour. The pharaoh was afraid that the rising population of the Jews would affect his throne, his race and his sacred religion.

By a royal proclamation the pharaoh decreed that all male children born of Jews should be killed as soon as they were born. He had special midwives who had to be at hand to stifle and kill the newborn. Abortion was unknown in those days, and if the midwives did not get there on time for the birth of a child then the babies who survived were killed by a special squad of soldiers. It was a horrible time in the history of the human race, when family planning and population control was practised by the government in the most inhumane manner. Imagine the terror and fear when an Israelite girl became pregnant — it was a nightmare. The pregnancy had to be concealed at all times, and when the baby had to be born then it had to be before the arrival of the midwife. Everything had to be done quickly and silently. They were slaves and lived in communes without any privacy.

As a gynaecologist who was running a maternity home I wonder how I managed with the sounds of the delivery room. These days we have state-of-the-art drugs and even epidurals to add to the comfort of those in labour.

Now, coming back to the story, the pharaoh was not the same one who gave all power to Joseph. "A new king, who knew nothing about Joseph, came to power in Egypt. He said to his people, 'These Israelites are so numerous and strong that they are a threat to us. In case of war they might join our enemies . . . '" That is why he made them slaves. He even instructed the midwives personally, and two midwives are mentioned by name — Shiphrah and Puah. He ordered them to, "Kill the baby if it is a boy; but if it is a girl, let it live".

Later, when he found out that the population of the Jews was still increasing, he issued a new command to all his people; "Take every new-born Hebrew boy and throw him into the Nile . . ." *(Exodus 1:22)*.

This was also a sad position for a certain Levite family. Amram was married to Jochebed, who was his auntie (his father's sister). They had two children, Miriam and Aaron. Jochebed was again pregnant and was hoping it would be a girl when this order came into force. But it was a baby boy. She delivered him quietly before the arrival the official Egyptian midwife. When she looked at the baby her heart melted and she decided to hide the baby. She was successful for three months. Then it became too risky. She realized that she could not keep the baby any longer. The only answer was to take the child to the River Nile. She made a basket of reeds and covered it with tar to make it waterproof. The idea was to allow the baby to drift away to some shore where, by the kindness of God, some kind soul would pity the cute baby and not leave it as food for the crocodiles.

The baby's sister, Miriam, must have been heartbroken to leave the scene and stood some distance away to see what would happen. A strange thing happened. Perhaps, it was providential. The daughter of the pharaoh "came down to the river to bathe, while her servants walked along the bank" *(Exodus 2:5)*.

The royal princess, perhaps the only daughter of the pharaoh, had no children. It is generally believed that she was a widow, because there is no mention of any husband. She could have been a spinster but that would put her in an older age-bracket. Most scholars believed that she made it to the Promised Land and so, with the wandering in the Sinai Desert for forty years, she must have been in her later twenties when she found the baby.

The good news is that she noticed the basket floating among the reeds. It must have appeared strange. What would the daughter of a pharaoh want with a basket among the reeds. She had all the wealth. What was a basket worth to her? However, she asked her servant, the slave girl, to fetch it. This must have been God's design. When the Hebrew slave saw what was in the basket she shouted, "This is one of the Hebrew babies".

The natural tendency of any Egyptian at that time was to take the baby and cast it into the River Nile. Trying to save the baby or harbouring it would be a crime against the state and the pharaoh.

But the pharaoh's daughter (call her Neferita) thought differently. There was something about the child that appealed to her. She decided to rescue the baby, and, more than that, went a step further by deciding to adopt the child as her own. What a woman! She, as the daughter of a pharaoh, could easily adopt any Egyptian child, but she made her choice and gave him a unique name — Moses (meaning out of the water). The child grew up with the real mother nursing him, thanks to Miriam. Moses became the greatest Hebrew, the Deliverer, who spoke face to face with God, and who brought the Israelites out of slavery. He is also the Law Giver. The pharaoh of the Exodus is believed to be Amenhotep II (reigned 1453 to 1419 BC).

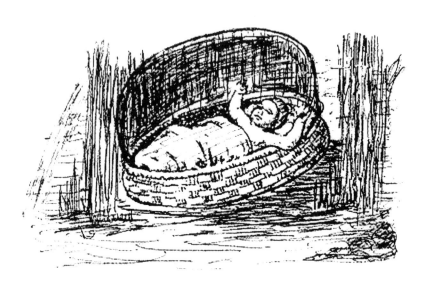

NODIAH (Hebrew: Encounter with Jehovah")
Nehemiah 6:14

Probably she was given a name to bring the girl in close contact with the Lord, but it did not turn out to be so. She chose the wrong path.

Nodiah became the nemesis of Nehemiah the good prophet. His Book is divided into four parts. The first part concerns his return from Babylonic captivity to Jerusalem. (The Persian Emperor sent him there to go and govern Judah.) The second part concerns the rebuilding of the walls of Jerusalem. The third concerns the solemn reading of the Law of God. The fourth deals with the activities of Nehemiah as Governor of Judah.

Artaxerxes was the Persian emperor who encouraged the Jews to return and Nehemiah to be appointed Governor of Judah. While Nehemiah was in Susa, the capital, he was the emperor's wine steward. One day, while he was waiting at the dinner table, attending to the emperor and the empress, his sad countenance caught the attention of these two very important people.

"Why are you looking so sad?" asked the emperor to Nehemiah. Then the wine steward related the sad state of Jerusalem with its broken gates and walls. The emperor was moved by his narration and gave him letters of introduction to other governors, to help him get timber from the royal forests, and also sent an army cavalry to accompany him. For twelve years he was the Governor of Judah as he feverishly worked on building the city.

But there was opposition. Nodiah and other prophets opposed him. They did not want the grandeur of Jerusalem to come to prominence once again. There were several plots by Nodiah, Sanballat, Tobiah and Geshem to bodily harm Nehemiah. There were poison letters from Sanballat and Nodiah and others, saying that Nehemiah was rebuilding the walls so as to get the Jewish people to revolt and that he would make himself king.

Nehemiah prayed daily seven times and implored the Lord. "God remember what Tobiah and Sanballat have done and punish them. Remember that woman Nodiah and all the other prophets who tried to frighten me". He was a very upright man who used prayer as his weapon. "Listen to them mocking us, O God. Let their ridicule fall on their own heads. . . . Don't forgive the evil they do and don't forget their sins, for they have insulted us who are building".

These like Nodiah and the other prophets, who insulted Nehemiah and who were thorns in his efforts of good work, are existent even today. We come across them in our daily lives. We try to do something good but there are those who work in the wrong direction to discourage us and slow us down. Who can help us? Only God. He will work through good people around us.

This is a good lesson in stress management. Stress is nothing new. It existed even in Paradise. Eve was so stressed that she decided to share her temptations with Adam. Together they committed the sin of disobedience.

In the world today the tempo of human activity has increased incredibly. There are myriad distractions and temptations. There are evil-doers who prey on unsuspecting individuals, cajoling them into committing crimes.

We need to identify the type of stressors and motivate ourselves in the right direction. Our best ally is God. Our best weapon of self-defence is prayer.

Think It Over:

If we have our ally in God, why do we need talismans and good-luck charms, tarot cards and horoscopes? To resort to these is to show distrust in God and His saving grace.

ORPAH (Gazelle)
Ruth 1:6-13

When I witnessed the Oprah Winfrey Show in Los Angeles, I was transported back in time to a certain scene in the Bible. It was to an obscure village in Moab, a region on the eastern front of Israel. She was a non-Hebrew young maid, and her husband, a son of Naomi, had died leaving her a widow. Yet another young widow who also originated from Moab was Ruth. Orpah is not such a well-known name in the Bible. There is hardly any mention of her. During one of my 'talks' at a Bible lecture someone even remarked that she symbolized "one who gave up a golden opportunity".

I would like to differ. To me Orpah represents the people who are unfortunate and who are naive. They plead and are rejected. They consequently move or retreat to willingly give up the challenge so that the other candidate may be successful. Somebody has to be the sacrificial lamb. Orpah made it easier for Ruth and Naomi to succeed. Thus her name disappeared in the eons of time. Then in the 21st Century this name became a household name thanks to the Queen of Talk Shows, the one and only Oprah Winfrey. I think the Biblical namesake would be very proud of her, considering the good work Oprah is doing fighting the cause of the unfortunates.

In the Bible, Naomi, fed up with the row of misfortunes bogging her down, decides to pack up and leave for Israel. She had lived in Moab with her two widowed daughters-in-law for ten years. It was extremely difficult for the two girls to return to their respective Moabite families. They decided to follow Naomi, their mother-in-law. Now visualize the three widows on their lonely journey back to Israel. Suddenly, Naomi gets a brainwave and she wonders what she could do with these two young, foreign, widows. So she asks them to go back to their family and people. Now, this is a very stressed woman speaking. There are tears and the girls plead to continue their journey with Naomi in vain. Finally, it seems that one has to give up. The graceful, beady-eyed, pretty girl decides to give up and take the lonely road back to Moab, thus making it easy for

Ruth to follow her mother-in-law.

Three is an odd number and is a crowd. It is perhaps, bad there are three women, and worse if it had to be three widows on a lonely road. Nobody knows the fate that awaited Orpah when she returned alone.

PEDROMA (Peter's Mother)

Matthew 8:14

Peter is somewhat special among the Apostles because of a few unique features. One feature I wish to highlight here is the fact that he had a mother-in-law. No other Apostle is recorded as being married or having a mother-in-law.

There is, however, no mention of Peter's wife. The mother-in-law must have been a good lady in the Gospel because she entertained them and offered hospitality to Jesus, the Apostles and the disciples.

The role of the mother-in-law is always a controversial one. She is the butt of many jokes. I've seen a few car bumper stickers displaying the mother-in-law in a sarcastic manner. One that my neighbour has, declares, *Ex-mother-in-law in the trunk*. Either it means that he got rid of the ex-wife's mother and stored her in the trunk of his car or it could be a warning to the present mother-in-law.

When Peter's mother-in-law had high fever, Peter implored Jesus to come and heal her and He came to perform the Divine Physician's job. Peter must have been very fond of her and she too reciprocated the special relationship. Today the house in Capernaum has been restored in her honour.

PHOEBE (Greek: Bright, Shining, Radiant)
(Spelt PHEBE — in King James Version)
Romans 16:1-2

Phoebe was a servant (worker) of the church in Cenchreae *(Romans 16:1-2)*. This setting takes place in a city close to Corinth, Greece, which was a centre of pagan idolatry. Paul, the self-proclaimed Apostle of Jesus Christ, on discovering that this place had a moral vacuum, was attracted to it like a moth to a flame. He set up an active church in this fishing port city about AD 51, with deacons. Phoebe was a deaconess.

Paul's message, reaching out to the people of Corinth, is as follows: "I recommend to you our sister Phoebe, who serves the church in Cenchreae. Receive her in the Lord's name, as God's people should, and give her any help she may need from you; for she herself has been a good friend to many people and also to me.

Paul was a very determined man, and one in a hurry to spread the Word of God to others. He needed good friends that he could rely on. Phoebe was one such person.

Corinth was a city that was famous for its temple prostitutes. Young virgins were recruited to serve in the pagan temple rituals. Sex was regarded as a sacred ritual. It was certainly an uphill task for Paul to preach against these unhappy practices and rescue women from unscrupulous men. In recent times in countries like Afghanistan the Taliban have reduced women to the level of sex slaves. In Thailand and South Africa this cult still exists and it extends to children. Sex with virgins is supposed to cure incurable diseases like AIDS. It does not!

POTIPHARINA (Potiphar's Wife)

(Also Potipha, Porina)
Genesis 39:7-19

Potipharina was an Egyptian, the wife of a high-ranking Egyptian official in pharaoh's court. He was the captain of the palace guard. She was not an important woman in the Bible, and we do not even know her real name, but she is the woman who accused Joseph of attempted rape and had him thrown in jail.

Joseph was the favourite son of Jacob. His mother was Rachel. His brothers were jealous of him and sold him to Midianite slave-traders. The brothers then faked a story that their brother was killed by wild animals. These traders sold Joseph to Potiphar. Joseph won great favour with the captain and became his personal servant. Potiphar's sensuous wife was physically attracted to this young man who was well built and handsome. She found him irresistibly attractive and made several sexual advances, all in vain. She even pleaded with him to go to bed with her but Joseph refused, saying, "Look, my master does not have to concern himself with anything in the house, because I am here. He has put me in charge of everything he has ... he has not kept back anything from me except you. How then could I do such an immoral thing and sin against God?"

Then, one day it happened. When Joseph was in the house attending to his duties she found the perfect opportunity, as there was no one else in the house including the servants (she must have sent them away on some errands). She came to Joseph and caught him by his robes and tried to pull him towards her. Joseph left the robe in her hands and ran away. She felt ashamed and shouted, "Look at this! This Hebrew that my husband brought to the house is insulting us. He came into my room and tried to rape me, but I screamed as loud as I could. When he heard me scream, he ran outside leaving his robe beside me". She kept the robe as evidence and told her husband the story of the attempted rape. Potiphar was obviously furious and had Joseph arrested and thrown into jail. But even in prison God was with Joseph. The jailor took a liking to Joseph and was kind to him. He put Joseph in charge of the other prisoners. Joseph was responsible for everything.

Joseph also built up quite a good reputation in prison as a dream interpreter. We know later how he won the pharaoh's favour and became the Prime Minister of Egypt. Potiphar's wife must have been sorry to see the young man decorated and win the pharaoh's favour. All this happened because Joseph was an upright person, morally sound and imploring God's mercy.

The Way to Heaven:

We cannot make it to Heaven without the help of God. Joseph's story illustrates that, in spite of odds and obstacles, God's saving grace will pull us through.

There is a story of a man who went up to Heaven and demanded to be sent inside the Pearly Gates. St Peter and the security guard told him that he was on the waiting list. He mentioned with protests all the good acts that would qualify him for immediate entry. No use. He finally make it when he begged for God's help and Divine Mercy.

Moral: If we make it there, it will be on God's Mercy-and-Saving-Grace Ticket.

134

PRISCILLA
Romans 16:3-5

"I send greetings to Priscilla and Aquila, my fellow-workers in the service of Christ Jesus; they risked their lives for me. I am grateful to them — not only I, but all the Gentile churches as well. Greetings also to the church that meets in their house. . . . Greetings also to Andronicus and Julia, fellow-Jews who were in prison with me; they are well known among the apostles, and they became Christians before I did".

Paul suffered imprisonment and even whipping for Jesus, his Master. His letter to the Romans outlines his gratefulness to these fellow-sufferers, who risked their lives to protect him and be seen with him. There were times when there was no church structure and he had gatherings in their houses.

Phoebe, Priscilla, Julia and others were early Christians, who gave witness to Christ fearlessly. Some were tortured and killed. The Church grew with the blood of these martyrs.

Think It Over:

The Church was built on the blood of the martyrs. How can you let them down? There are religions which are easy to follow; Christianity is not one of these convenient religions. Christianity is perhaps more demanding and following it can make you more pure of mind and heart.

Dr G. Reth

QUEEN OF SHEBA
1 Kings 10:1-13

Ask any Ethiopian and he will tell you that the name of the Queen of Sheba is Balkis. She was the undisputed leader of a powerful empire that traded with many countries. The items she traded were gold, cereals, spices, perfumes and incense. She heard of King Solomon and his great wisdom. Seeing is believing, so she journeyed to Jerusalem to see him and learn something from him. Earlier, she had been considered the wisest woman ruler, now she had to meet the best.

"The Queen of Sheba heard of Solomon's fame, and she travelled to Jerusalem to test him with difficult questions. She brought with her a large group of attendants, as well as camels loaded with spices, jewels, and a large amount of gold. When she and Solomon met, she asked him all the questions that she could think of. He answered them all; there was nothing too difficult for him to explain."

Today archeologists have worked in the regions of Yemen and discovered the ancient city of Saba (pronounced similarly to Sheba). There are dams, a fortress and sun-temple pillars, all indicating a very well-structured kingdom. This kingdom stretched across the East African coast and was at that time the territory of Abyssinia. Later on it became Ethiopia and Eritrea.

Coffee was also one of their principal crops, and who does not know the real name of coffee — café Arabica? It was special here because of the dry highland climate. If you like Mocha coffee, you probably need to know that a city still exists in Yemen called Mocha. By the way, the only country in the world to have a national flag with the coffee plant is the country of Yemen.

When the Queen of Sheba came to Jerusalem she came to establish bilateral trade relations and also learn about the Jewish culture and religion.

When she saw the food that was served, the living quarters for his officials, the palace staff and the uniforms they wore, the feasts and the sacrifices he offered in the Temple, it left her breathless and amazed.

It also sounds like the Corrs — the pretty girls who sing: "Go on leave me breathless". She also had a child by Solomon. She went back to her city full of praises to the God of Solomon. She prayed thus: "Praise the Lord your God! He has shown how pleased He is with you by making you King of Israel. Because his love for Israel is eternal, he has made you their king so that you can maintain law and justice".

Ethiopian history has it that she was succeeded by her son who was Jewish. Later on Christianity came to take a firm root in the religion of the country, but the Ethiopian Jews still maintained their identities. They are called Falashas and have been directly included into the Israelite Army and workforce. They are also called the Black Jews or Ethiopian Jews. All this came about thanks to the Queen of Sheba.

There is an interesting item I wish to record here in this book. This is based on the information given to me by a very high-ranking official in Emperor Haile Selassie's court. When the Emperor was overthrown, he abdicated. This official settled down in Los Angeles. He was my patient and a very good man — deeply religious. I stayed with him for a few months and during this time he told me extensively about the Ark of the Covenant. This Ark with the stone tablets went missing from the Temple of Jerusalem. When the Temple was looted several times the Ark was taken to protected underground chambers known only to a few, so it escaped the ransacking by the Assyrians and the Babylonic captivity. It was there when Jesus Christ was preaching in Jerusalem. Herod the Great rebuilt the second Temple to be more magnificent than that of Solomon.

The Ark was taken to Ethiopia before Titus and the Roman legion came to Jerusalem in AD 70 to raze the city to the ground and the Temple too. Only the Western or Wailing Wall remains.

The escapade of the Ark of the Covenant is what I refer to as the Ethiopian Connection. Every year, more than in any other place on earth, the Ethiopians piously celebrate the feast of the Ark of the Covenant with processions and covenant boxes. The Ark is in Ethiopia. A high-ranking Ethiopian minister of Haile Selassie told me so.

Once again, all this would not have happened if the Queen of Sheba did not visit Solomon and establish a relationship with him.

RACHEL (See also under Leah) (Hebrew, Ewe)
Genesis 29 9-13

While Jacob was still talking with them, Rachel arrived with the flock. When Jacob saw Rachel with his uncle Laban's flock, he went to the well, rolled the stone back, and watered the sheep. Then he kissed her and began to cry for joy. He told her, "I am your father's relative, the son of Rebecca".

Jacob was asked by his father, Isaac, to go to Mesopotamia to look for a wife from his own family. Laban, the son of Bethuel, the brother of Rebecca, lived there in Haran. For Jacob it was love at first sight. He went to meet Rachel's father and ask for her hand.

Laban had two daughters: the older was Leah and the younger Rachel, who was more shapely and beautiful. Jacob put a proposal to Laban that he would work for seven years, "if you will let me marry Rachel". Laban was happy and agreed. Time flew past through the seven years and Jacob worked hard to please his prospective father-in-law. At the end of seven years he reminded Laban of his promise to give his daughter. So Laban threw a wedding feast and invited everyone. Jacob and Rachel were married in style. Then at night Laban slipped Leah into the honeymoon bed instead of Rachel. Jacob had intercourse with Leah that night. "Not until the next morning did Jacob discover it was Leah".

An angry Jacob went up to Laban, "I worked to get Rachel. Why have you tricked me?" Laban gave his excuses and demanded that he would give Rachel if he promised to work for another seven years. After the wedding celebrations were over Laban gave Rachel to him on the condition he enforced.

There was enough tension in that family involving the two sisters and their maids. Jacob had more than his share of wives. That is how we learn that Jacob had his twelve sons and one daughter, Dinah. This girl was raped by Shechem.

Rachel died after a difficult childbirth near Bethlehem and was buried by the road side. The baby boy's name was Benjamin. There is a memorial stone placed by Jacob that still stands there till the present day.

RAHAB (Hebrew: Proud)
Joshua 2:1-21, Hebrews 11:31

Her name features in the capture and the fall of Jericho. The gates and walls of Jericho were strong and these kept the Israelites out. Israelites with Joshua commanding them took the Covenant Box and marched several times as directed by the Lord with the sounding of trumpets and loud shouting.

"The city and everything in it must be totally destroyed as an offering to the Lord. Only the prostitute Rahab and her household will be spared, because she hid our spies," ordered Joshua. The walls collapsed. With their swords they killed men and women, young and old. They also killed the cattle, the sheep and the donkeys.

Joshua ordered his special force, "Go into the prostitute's house and bring her and her family out, as you promised her". So Rahab's family (her father, mother, her brothers and the rest of her family) and her slaves were taken to safety. "Her descendants have lived in Israel to this day".

Rahab did something that brought her to be the pride of the Israelites. She had a low standing in Jericho and was considered a prostitute. But the Israelites found that this beautiful lady had a good family and was willing to worship the true God. She was willing to risk her life and that of her family members by siding with the Israelites. She made a deal with them that if she helped them then they should spare her family. She hung a red cord on her window to indicate her house to the Israelites.

The rulers of Jericho sought her for her information about the spies but she lied to them. She lowered the spies out through her window. Evidently, she was known to the King of Jericho for he asked her "The men in your house have come to spy out the whole country! Bring them out!" She hid them under stalks of flax in the roof and told the king a different direction that they had taken.

She also showed her faith and belief in the Lord of the Israelites. "I know that the Lord has given you this land. . . . We have heard how the Lord dried up the Red Sea infront of you when you were

139

leaving Egypt". She was certainly well informed and she narrated these and other incidents to the spies as they spent the night hiding from the king and the army.

She risked her life and chose the right army. If they lost, she would have lost. But she had her faith in the True God. She went to live in Canaan, the Promised Land.

The Canaanites:

The land of Canaan was the Promised Land. Abraham made a special sacrifice and was told by God that the land would be his (Abraham's).

Canaan is a fertile area with valleys and rolling green hills on the slopes of which grow olive groves. To the Israelites, who were starved and parched in the Sinai Desert for forty years, Canaan was a paradise — a garden in which to put all their hopes and future — the Promised Land indeed.

The land was named after the wayward grandson of Noah who was not favoured by God. Consequently, the people, Canaanites, descendants of Canaan, were not on good terms with the Israelites. They had many gods. The chief god was Baal, the weather god. Another was the goddess Asherah (Astarte), the goddess of war and fertility.

The people were — Hittites, Hivites, Perizzites, Girgashites, Amorites and the Jebusites (of Jerusalem).

REBECCA (Hebrew: Faithful)
Genesis 24:15-34

Rebecca was the wife of Isaac — the son of Abraham and Sarah.

The Bible tells us they were a lovely couple. She was very beautiful, yet for twenty years they were childless. Isaac was prayerful and reminded God of how He promised to make Abraham's children so numerous that they would make a great nation.

Abraham felt he was very old and needed a wife for Isaac and he wanted to choose only one from his own people.

So he told his trusted servant to go to northern Mesopotamia where he originated and look for a suitable wife. The servant went there and, while resting near a well, he prayed for a good partner for Isaac.

"Before he had finished praying, Rebecca arrived with a water-jar on her shoulder".

She was the daughter of Bethuel (Rethuel), who was the son of Abraham's brother Nahor and his wife Milcah. The servant immediately put a nose ring in her nose and bracelets on her arms when she introduced herself.

She took them to her father Bethuel and mother Milcah and brother Laban. They introduced themselves and exchanged gifts. Soon she returned with her camels and her servants to Isaac's camp.

Isaac was forty years old when he married Rebecca. Isaac's mother had died meanwhile and did not get to meet Rebecca. When Rebecca became pregnant she experienced a "struggle" in her womb. She had a twin pregnancy. She asked God, "Why should something like this happen to me?"

The Lord said to Rebecca, "Two nations are within you; You will give birth to two rival peoples. One will be stronger than the other; the older will serve the younger".

The elder of the twins was hairy and he was named Esau. The second was holding on to Esau's heel so was called Jacob (meaning heel in Hebrew). Isaac was sixty years old when they were born.

"Isaac preferred Esau, because he enjoyed eating the animals

141

Esau killed, but Rebecca preferred Jacob" *(Genesis 25:27-28)*. Esau was a skilled hunter and loved the outdoors, but Jacob was a quiet man who stayed at home.

Esau, when he was forty, married two foreign wives, who were Hittites. This displeased Isaac because his father had been wholly committed to getting a wife from his own people. His mother also despised the foreign wives: "They made life miserable for Isaac and Rebecca" *(Genesis 26:34-35)*.

When Isaac was old and became blind he sent for his eldest son, Esau. He wanted him to go and hunt and cook the animal meat for him. "Cook me some of that tasty food that I like. . . . I will give you my final blessing before I die".

Rebecca overheard this conversation between father and son and called in Jacob and gave him instructions. "Now my son," Rebecca said, "listen to me and do what I say. Go to the flock and pick out two fat young goats . . . " She said she would do the cooking and "make some of that food your father likes so much".

Jacob told his mother that though blind his father would be able to identify the son by the sense of touch. (Esau was hairy.) So his mother did the needful. She put on Jacob his brother Esau's best clothes and the skin of goats to resemble a hairy person. In this encounter Rebecca was really smart, because she even made Isaac smell like his brother to be sure.

"Come closer and kiss me, my son". As he came up to kiss him, Isaac smelled his clothes — so he gave Jacob his blessing.

Isaac said, "The pleasant smell of my son is like the smell of a field which the Lord has blessed". Then he gave him his special blessings which he ended with the words, "May those who curse you be cursed, and may those who bless you be blessed".

Earlier, in another incident, Esau was very hungry and asked for the red bean (lentil) soup that Jacob was cooking. "I'm starving; give me some of that red stuff". (This is why the Edom (Edomites) are so called — because it means red). Jacob asked him to give up his rights as the first born for the soup. Esau readily gave this for the soup and some bread. "That was all Esau cared about his rights as the first-born son" *(Genesis 25:34)*.

He never considered that one day it would matter very much to be the leader of the nation. When Esau found out that he had been cheated by Jacob he said, "This is the second time that he has cheated me. No wonder his name is Jacob". Then he hated his brother. When Rebecca heard of Esau's plans to kill his brother, she sent for Jacob and asked him to leave for her brother's house in Haran. Laban would look after him.

Rebecca said to Isaac, "I am sick and tired of Esau's foreign wives. If Jacob also marries one of these Hittite girls, I might as well die". So Isaac called Jacob and advised him not to marry any foreign wives. "Go . . . to the home of your grandfather Bethuel, and marry one of the girls there, one of your uncle Laban's daughters. May Almighty God bless your marriage and give you many children, so that you will become the father of many nations!"

Esau meanwhile went to meet Ishmael, son of Abraham and Hagar, and married his daughter Mahalath.

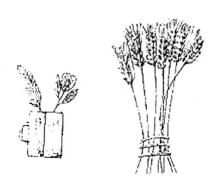

REVELON (Woman of the Revelation)
Revelation 12:1-18

The Book of Revelation is the last Book of the Holy Bible. It was written by the Evangelist John, in the island of Patmos, to where he had been banished.

Christianity at that time was firmly rooted in Asia Minor and the seven Churches of the region were administered with Ephesus as the epicentre. John was looked upon as a threat to the other religions and so he was sent away. The other Apostles were by this time already martyred. John was special. He was spared from harsh persecution by the grace of Jesus Christ, the Lord.

To understand John and his contributions I undertook a long and tedious journey to Asia Minor and managed to visit the churches he helped to establish with Paul in particular. John's tomb is still there in Ephesus, in present-day Turkey, in a ruined church that bears his name. It is a huge cathedral with marble columns and the restoration process is evident with a board indicating the efforts of the University of Ohio at Lima.

The Book was written at a time when the Church was severely persecuted. The style of writing is entirely apocryptical. There are hidden meanings with metaphors and symbols, which have been variously interpreted.

In the first chapter, which is the introduction, these words appear: "Happy is the one who reads this book, and happy are those who listen to the words of this prophetic message and obey what is written in this book!"

There are several visions John received and he mentions one very intriguing one entitled "The Woman and the Dragon" *(Revelation 12:1-18)*.

The lady mentioned here is the good person who gave birth to a son who would make good changes in the world. The huge dragon is also called "the serpent called the Devil, or Satan, that deceived the whole world". The dragon represents all the evil forces at work and is one that, "is filled with rage".

There seems to be a reference here to Mary the mother of Jesus as she had to flee from Jerusalem to Antioch and then to Ephesus. Our Lord, dying on the cross, entrusted His mother Mary to John the Evangelist. He took her on his journeys, safe from the evil forces that killed her Son and the other Apostles. She died in Ephesus and there is a house on the mountain that bears her name that is believed by the Churches and the Vatican and archeologists and the University of Ohio to be the last house of the Virgin Mary. I went to this house which is now reconstructed as a Byzantine chapel and is in the custody of the Vincentian Fathers. A devout American Christian, George Quatman, is mainly responsible for the restoration and upkeep. His Foundation initiated the process to make the place a holy site. The Turkish authorities however collect toll from the pilgrims who visit the last house of the Virgin Mary or Merem Ana Evi at Panalakaulupu (the sacred mound). Strangely, the visions of Anne Catherine Emmerich helped locate this house.

The woman in the Book of Revelation is described as one "whose dress was the sun and who had the moon under her feet and a crown of twelve stars on her head".

While on the Book of Revelation let me add that the Book also condemns the city of Babylon — that great city is personified as a woman and in Revelation, 17:1-18 is called the "famous prostitute". There are several gross descriptions of her.

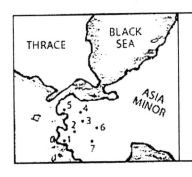

The Seven Churches of Asia Minor
1. Ephesus (main church)
2. Smyrna
3. Sardis
4. Thyatira
5. Pergamum
6. Philadelphia
7. Laodicea

RHODA (Greek: From Rhodes)
Acts 12:12-14

King Herod persecuted the early Church. He had James, the brother of John, sentenced to death by beheading. Peter was arrested and put in prison with chains. There were two guards posted to look after him, but the angel of the Lord appeared and saved him. Peter went to the house of Mary, the mother of John Mark. "Peter knocked at the outside door, and a servant-girl named Rhoda came to answer it. She recognized Peter's voice and was so happy that she ran back in without opening the door, and announced that Peter was standing outside." They were amazed to see him as they were sure Herod would behead him too. Peter explained to them how "the Lord had brought him out of prison". Herod had planned to put him on public trial after the Passover feast. The people of the church were praying for him.

He walked out of the prison, guided by the angel of the Lord, up to the last iron gate leading to the outside of the city. He went straight to the house of one of the faithful whom he could trust. They were overjoyed and amazed. Rhoda was no ordinary servant. She was a believer and she knew Peter by his voice — even behind the closed door. She ran back without opening the door and announced that Peter was standing outside. "You are mad!" the others in the house said to her. But she insisted that it was true. It was Peter. They thought it was an angel, and it could not be Peter. But it was true. He gave them some instructions and left, lest they be in trouble.

Next day there was confusion in the prison. Herod was furious and sent out search parties to arrest Peter. Herod questioned the guards and put them to death.

Herod Agrippa I, ruler of Galilee, died shortly after this incident, "when an angel of the Lord struck Herod down . . . He was eaten by worms and died".

RUFINA (Mother of Rufus)
Romans 16:13-14

"I send greetings to Rufus, that outstanding worker in the Lord's service, and to his mother, who has always treated me like a son".

These are the greeting words of St Paul in his letter to the Romans, where he gave instructions to keep watch over those who caused divisions in the Church. He had by then established churches all over Asia Minor and in Rome too. There were good workers who showed kindness and love to Paul, who was nearing the end of his apostolic mission. Rufus' mother had been like a mother to him. They were touched by his simplicity, his eagerness to spread the Word of God in strange lands with such risk. After Paul's death by beheading through an execution order, it is the faith and goodwill of good folk that kept the gospel flourishing

Perhaps, this is to be viewed as two awards of appreciation from Paul to the Romans. In the first, Rufus is given the category "outstanding worker". The second award is given to the mother of Rufus. You probably have seen even in restaurants pictures of the "outstanding worker" of the month.

From time to time we need to appreciate those who do good deeds or outstanding service. This gives a morale boost to the worker.

But in this case Paul gives credit to Rufina for looking after him tenderly and with the love of a good mother. She too was in the Lord's service and is appreciated — for all time — even in Heaven.

Think It Over:

Make hay while the sun shines. Make use of the talents that you have. You have one life and you must make the best use of it, to glorify Him who sent you into this world to perform.

Dr G. Reth

147

RUTH (Hebrew: Vision of Beauty)
Ruth 1-4

The story of Ruth and references to her are in the Book of Ruth, which is placed between the Book of Judges and the First Book of Samuel. It is narrated in four chapters — Ruth I to Ruth IV. The first chapter deals with Ruth making her entry into Bethlehem with Naomi. The second and third deal with the meeting with Boaz. The fourth deals with her marriage to Boaz.

The narrative is interesting and peaceful, unlike the book prior to it which is full of violence. The Book of Samuel is also a record of turbulent times when the Ark of the Covenant was captured from Shiloh by the Philistines and Eli's two sons are killed in the battle. Even Eli dies tragically.

In the story of Ruth there is love and romance. In the Books of Judges and Samuel, disaster comes when people turn away from God. In Ruth we see a foreigner getting blessed because of her steadfast faith in the God of Israel. She becomes an Israelite and adopts the customs and traditions, and God truly blesses her and her lineage. She becomes the great-grandmother of Israel's greatest king, namely David, and puts Bethlehem on the map for all time. Down the line comes Jesus Christ, who is a descendant of David, and who was born in Bethlehem. Ruth was a Moabite from the land on the eastern aspect of Israel. Moabites have their own rituals and gods. When there was a famine in Bethlehem and in parts of Judah, Naomi and her husband Elimelech along with their two sons, Mahlon and Chilion, went to Moab. But disaster struck and Naomi's husband died, soon followed by the two sons. The sons had married two local Moabite girls, Ruth and Orpah. Now Naomi, a widow, was left with two widows.

Naomi heard reports that life was good and crops were plenty in Bethlehem. She decided to go back to her land. She was old; her sons had been married for ten years, without any children.

She took her foreign daughters-in-law and started on the journey homeward. On the way, Naomi changed her mind and told the girls to go home to their mothers. But the girls cried and begged to stay with her (see Naomi, page 121). Finally Orpah left tearfully but Ruth refused to go and held on to her.

In Bethlehem when they arrived it was the time of the wheat and barley harvest. Ruth took it upon herself to work in the fields gathering the grain left behind by the workers. She did not know the fields belonged to Boaz. One day while she was working Boaz came and he was told about her by the workers. He gave her advice and permission to work in the fields.

Ruth bowed down with her face touching the ground and said to Boaz, "Why should you be so concerned about me? Why should you be so kind to a foreigner?" When Boaz gave her his reasons, Ruth remarked, "You are very kind to me, sir. You have made me feel better by speaking gently to me, even though I am not the equal of one of your servants".

Boaz allowed her to eat with his other workers. Then he did something extraordinary. He noticed how hard-working poor Ruth was, so he asked his steward to take some of the collected barley and wheat from the bundles and leave it out on the ground for her to pick up. Now, to cut a long story short, eventually Boaz and Ruth were married. It was her obedience to her mother-in-law and her good nature that won her recognition.

Boaz remarked just before deciding to marry her, "Now don't worry, Ruth. I will do everything you ask; as everyone in town knows, you are a fine woman". Boaz was a true gentleman. He convened a meeting of elders and even a relative of Naomi's husband was present. He was given the first chance to bid in the land sale and marry Ruth, but he backed off. He offered his sandals to Boaz — a custom in those days to declare a person's withdrawal.

The story of Ruth and Boaz is a love story and one with a happy ending. She indeed must have been a wonderful and beautiful woman to have captured the hearts of so many including that of the rich man Boaz. Her son Obed was the father of Jesse the father of King David.

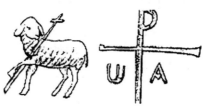

SALOME (Hebrew: Shalom Peace)

Mark 15:40-41; 16:1-2

"Women of Jerusalem! Don't cry for me, but for yourselves and your children. For the days are coming when people will say, 'How lucky are the women who never had children' . . . " *(Luke 23:29-31).*

Jesus gave a short speech to the women of Jerusalem with the words above. Jesus had to carry a large cross on his shoulders. The whole scene looked very pathetic. He had already been tortured, beaten, and whipped according to the orders of Pontius Pilate. Pilate ordered a special whipping so that the crowd would see Him so miserable they would pity Him and let Him go.

"Now I have examined Him here in your presence, and I have not found Him guilty of any of the crimes you accuse Him of. Nor did Herod find Him guilty, for he sent Him back to us. There is nothing this man has done to deserve death. So I will have Him whipped and let Him go".

One more time, because the people were chanting to free Barabas the murderer, Pilate asked the angry demonstrators. "But what crime has He committed?" Pilate said to them for the third time. "I cannot find anything He has done to deserve death! I will have Him whipped and set Him free."

Pilate was under tremendous pressure and great stress and that is why he buckled and gave in to the crowd. After all, one Jew dead is one less problem for the Romans!

The women who awaited the trial decision and who walked with Jesus were "weeping and wailing for Him". It is for this reason that Jesus gave the women of Jerusalem a short address. One of these holy women was Saloma.

Her name is specifically mentioned twice. She was also at the foot of the Cross with Mary the mother of Jesus and the other holy women. Mark mentions that these holy women had followed Jesus while He was in Galilee and had helped Him. "[Mary and the] other women who had come to Jerusalem with Him were there also" *(Mark 15:40-41).*

After the Sabbath was over, following the burial of Jesus, Mary Magdalene, Mary the mother of James, and Salome bought spices to go and anoint the body of Jesus". They went there early on Sunday morning — at sunrise. On the way these three women were worried about the large stone covering the tomb. They said to one another "Who will roll away the stone for us from the entrance to the tomb?"

We must place on record the faithfulness, courage and love that moved these three women to go to the tomb early that morning. They had cried all night — and probably did not sleep at all — with just one thought: To go to the tomb of Jesus and anoint his body. After all, it was a hurried burial because of the Passover restrictions. They were so helpless.

Matthew, in fact, in his Gospel mentions the women sat facing the tomb. Joseph of Arimathea placed the body of Jesus in the tomb he had recently dug out of solid rock and he rolled the large stone across the tomb. He did this and walked away but Mary Magdalene and the other women sat there facing the tomb for some hours.

Matthew also mentions that the chief priests and Pharisees met with Pilate and asked for the tomb to be guarded carefully until the third day so that the disciples would not be able to go and steal the body. Pilate obliged because he did not want any further trouble.

"Take a guard; go and make the tomb as secure as you can," Pilate ordered. So a seal was placed on the stone and an armed guard was left on duty. This was something serious and nobody could mess with the Roman authority. Imagine now the shock and stress on the three worn out, tired, sad ladies. As they came to the tomb, "Suddenly there was a violent earthquake . . . " Mary, Salome and the other Mary (Clopas) panicked. The angel rolled the stone away and sat on it.

The guards — there were two of them on duty — "were so afraid that they trembled and became like dead men".

The angel spoke to Salome and the other two women, "You must not be afraid," he said. "I know you are looking for Jesus, who was crucified. He is not here; He has been raised, just as He said. Come here and see the place where He was lying. Go quickly now, and tell His disciples . . . now He is going to Galilee".

So the three ladies, happy but terrified, left the tomb in a hurry — "afraid and yet filled with joy" according to Matthew, 28:8-9.

151

Now comes the big surprise. I believe Matthew because he is a learned Jew — he knew what he was writing a record for posterity. Jesus must have seen the joy and panic in the three women. (I do not think Jesus appeared only to Mary Magdalene, as some writers claim, as the trio were there.) "Suddenly Jesus met them [the two Marys and Salome] and said, 'Peace be with you'." They were excited to see the Lord again. Alive! He has come back to life! What a triumph of Good over Evil! What a victory! What a miracle — a man comes to life by His own power! Only GOD can do that. Jesus proved beyond all doubt that He is the Lord and God of all!

The women were overcome with emotion. "They came up to Him, took hold of His feet, and worshipped him". One could imagine their utterances. (Thomas is immortalized for his utterance, "My Lord and my God !")

What about the women? They worshipped Him. "You are God, You are the greatest. You did it as you said . . . Oh my God! Oh my God . . . !"

"Do not be afraid," Jesus said to them. "Go and tell my brothers [disciples] to go to Galilee, and there they will see me".

Jesus after His resurrection made only selected appearances. He had nothing more to prove to the usual crowd. Anyway, He had done enough already. Now these women — Salome and the two Marys — were the luckiest. They were the first witnesses!

152

SALOME, DAUGHTER OF HERODIAS

(Aramaic: Shalom, Peace)
Matthew 14:6-12

There is this question about the other Salome. Why was this gracious lady's name not that famous? She is recorded as being at the foot of the Cross when Jesus was dying and she was a witness to His resurrection — among the first three to see Him at the tomb.

The reason being, it was associated with a very bad girl named Salome. She was the daughter of Herodias, a woman of loose morals, who was the wife of Herod's brother (but married Herod later).

John the Baptist in his preaching stood out as a religious reformer and a very outspoken one. He mentioned that what Herod did was wrong and that he was living in sin with his sister-in-law. The daughter was a chip off the old block. A bad tree bears bad fruits, Jesus taught, and a good tree bears only good fruits. Jesus often spoke using such metaphors. Salome, daughter of Herodias, was one bad fruit.

Herod had eyes for Salome because she was young and beautiful. Herodias was even willing to give her daughter to Herod to please him and consolidate her position. She was evil. To prove her evilness she even allowed her daughter to entertain Herod when he threw a big banquet for his rich friends. At that party this wicked daughter of Herodias danced so seductively that it pleased Herod so much he was willing to give her anything, even half the kingdom.

The crafty, manipulative, evil woman, Herodias, used her trump card and told her daughter to ask for "the head of John the Baptist on a dish". And that is what she received.

What an evil family! She deserved an instant passport to Hell along with her mother and uncle. What a sad death for John, the first cousin of Jesus! A fancy, selfish request from a woman, and a ruler consents to the murder of an innocent man of God.

SAMARIWEL (Samirani, the Samaritan Woman at the Well)
John 4:5-30

Samariwel was the Samaritan lady at Jacob's well. This well is still there and it is close to the Samaritan town of Sychar. Jacob gave the field and the well to Joseph his son.

Jesus, tired from His travelling by land, walking with His apostles and disciples, sat down by the well. A beautiful Samaritan woman came to draw water and Jesus said to her, "Give me a drink of water". At that time the disciples and entourage had gone to town to buy food. The woman was taken aback as Samaritans were despised by the Jews. Jesus went on to tell her about His "life-giving water".

"Sir," the woman replied, "you haven't got a bucket, and the well is deep. Where would you get that life-giving water?"

Jesus said the water would quench thirst for all time.

"Sir, give me that water! Then I will never be thirsty again, nor will I have to come here to draw water".

Jesus answered, "Go and call your husband".

The woman replied, "I haven't got a husband".

Jesus answered, "You are right when you say you haven't got a husband. You have been married to five men, and the man you live with now is not really your husband. You have told me the truth".

The woman was shocked and recognized him as a holy man. "I see you are a prophet, sir".

The conversation went on till Jesus made an extraordinary effort to reveal His identity to her — directly. This is highly unusual but Jesus chose to tell a sinner and a stranger and an outcast who He really was. "I am He [the Messiah], I who is talking to you."

His disciples returned and saw Him talking to this stranger. But, none of them questioned Him or the woman. She left immediately, but left behind the water jar. She went to the town and started advertising for Jesus. "Come and see the man who told me everything I have ever done. Could He be the Messiah?" They came and Jesus stayed there for two days. Many were converted, thanks to her initiative.

SAPPHIRA (Greek: Sapphire)

Acts 5:3-4

In the Book the Acts of the Apostles, we learn that there was a fund to help meet the needs of the apostles. The believers sold their possessions and brought these to the apostles. Nobody forced anyone to sell part or all of their properties. They could declare what they had and give it to the apostles. "Those who owned fields or houses would sell them, bring the money received from the sale, and hand it over to the apostles". The money was distributed according to the needs of the people.

Now Ananias and his wife Sapphira too sold their property, but Ananias with his wife's agreement kept a part of the money for himself and gave some to the apostles. He had declared that he had given all to God.

This was wrong. This was a lie. So Peter asked, "Ananias, why did you let Satan take control of you and make you lie to the Holy Spirit . . . ? You have not lied men — you have lied to God." Ananias heard this and collapsed — dead. The young men came, wrapped up his body and buried him. His wife, Sapphira, did not know about it. Three hours later his wife came in and told Peter that she and her husband had sacrificed everything for God. Peter was ready to put her to the test. He asked her if it was the full amount and she declared it was so. He then mentioned that her husband too had lied and was struck down. He had just been buried. Now with her lies she would be next. On hearing this news she fell down and lay motionless — dead.

Such was the fear among the early Christians of lying to the Lord. Even today we know we can fool some people some of the time but we cannot fool everyone all the time. Most of all we can never ever fool God.

SHUNEMA (The Shunem Lady)

2 Kings 4:8-37

Elisha, the prophet who succeeded Elijah, used to go to Shunem, where a rich woman lived. Very often she invited him and his helper, Gehazi, to stay at her house. She would prepare meals and attend to all their needs without accepting any payment.

She once told her husband that since Elisha was a holy man it would be better to build a special room on the roof of our house for him. Then they decorated and furnished this room for his use.

One day Elisha decided to do something for this woman, in order to repay her for her generosity. "Ask her what I can do for her in return for all the trouble she has had in providing for our needs". Elisha was prepared to go and meet King Jehoshaphat of Judah and ask for a favour for her or from any high-ranking official. The lady replied that she was very well off and did not need anything.

Elisha found out that the rich couple had no children and that they were also very old. So he called her and gave her the good news, "By this time next year you will be holding a son in your arms".

Shunema laughed at this possibility. "Please, sir," she exclaimed, "don't lie to me You are a man of God!" However, a year later she gave birth to a son, proving nothing is impossible to God.

When the boy was still young he developed a headache and died. The mother carried the boy to Elisha's room and went quickly to search for the prophet on Mount Carmel. The prophet came and restored the boy back to life.

Goodness begets goodness. However rich one is, it is important that charity is practised. In times of need it is the kindness we show to others that comes back as kindness to us.

Nothing comes from nothing. Nothing ever could. Somewhere in your youth or childhood, you must have done something good. That will win you graces and goodwill from others.

TABITHA (Gazelle)
Acts 9:36-42

Peter travelled everywhere in the region of Asia Minor and worked miracles in the name of the Lord. In Joppa there was a woman named Tabitha (her Greek name was Dorcas, meaning Gazelle). She was a firm believer in the Lord. "She spent all her time doing good and helping the poor". She had a tremendous reputation similar to Mother Theresa — helper of those in distress. She became very ill and died. Her body was washed and laid in state for the believers to pay their respects. When the believers in Joppa heard that Peter was in Lydda (these places are nearby) they sent two representatives to Peter to ask him to come urgently. When he reached the house there was loud moaning in the room upstairs. The widows crowded around him, crying and showing him all the clothes that Dorcas had made while she was alive.

Peter was moved by what he saw. He knelt down and prayed after he had asked them all to move out of the room. Then he turned to the dead body and said, "Tabitha, get up!"

The dead woman opened her eyes and looked at Peter. She sat up. Peter reached over and helped her to her feet. Then he called all the believers to come in and gave Dorcas to them.

This was too much for the people. The news of her resurrection spread all over the region. Many new believers entered the fold. Peter stayed on teaching in Joppa for many days with Simon, the leather tanner, who lived by the seaside.

This miracle reinforced the faith the people had that Peter was a close follower of Jesus Christ. He had a special status among the apostles, in fact he was their leader. He must have implored Jesus, his Master, for a big favour and the Master obliged.

Evidently, she must have been worth it, because she is described as being not only a believer but a disciple of Jesus Christ. She is also a lady who worked tirelessly for the Lord — always doing good. She must have also been a lady with a good social standing to be able to make and distribute clothes to the needy. There must be many more charitable deeds this wonderful lady did that God recognized, and so He approved Peter's request to give her a new lease of life.

TALITHA AND TABLEDA

(Aramaic: Talitha, Little Girl/Tableda, Bleeding Lady)
Luke 8:40-56

The healing of Jairus' daughter is mentioned in Matthew 9:18-26, Mark 5:21-43 and Luke 8:40-56. It is important because it involved a high-ranking synagogue official's daughter. These Pharisees were generally against Jesus. But when illness strikes one who is of our own family, then we are willing to sacrifice everything to get a cure. In this case the girl became so critically ill that she died of the disease. Everyone knew she was dead, still the official "threw himself at Jesus' feet and begged Him to go to his home because his only daughter, who was twelve years old was dying".

There was a large crowd, and among the crowd was a woman who had suffered from bleeding for twelve years. She had spent all she had on doctors, but no one was able to cure her.

She was cured by Our Lord who performed a miracle by divine intervention. She was Tableda. Earlier she was just a nameless woman in the crowd — one of the crowd — but she had tremendous faith in Jesus. When all human effort failed it is wise to seek supernatural help. Perhaps it had to be that way. She and the other unbelievers would only then realize that it was a genuine miracle, medically certified as being a disease that is incurable — a condition that can be cured only by God. She had already endured the pain, suffering, and expenses for twelve long years. She now came from behind inching her way closer and closer to get near Jesus. 'If I just touch his clothes, I will get well'. She finally managed to touch the hem of the cloak of Jesus.

Jesus immediately reacted, "'Who touched me?' Everyone denied it . . . " *(Luke 8:45)*.

Imagine everyone asking themselves, 'Who touched Him? Not me! Could I get into trouble if I say I touched him?' So everyone denied any wrongdoing.

Peter, being the usual spokesman, decided to be bold and asked "Master, the people are all around you and crowding in on you."

But Jesus wanted them to know that He feels it when you speak to Him or manage to touch Him. "Someone touched me, for I knew it when power went out of me," Jesus said.

The woman realized that she had been found out, so she came trembling and fell at the feet of Jesus. Then she told Him why she had touched Him and how she was healed at once.

Jesus said to her, "My daughter, your faith has made you well. Go in peace".

Whilst Jesus was saying this a messenger came from the house of Jairus, "Your daughter has died," he told Jairus; "don't bother the Teacher any longer".

Jesus reassured Jairus; "Don't be afraid; only believe . . . " Then He did not allow anyone except Peter and James and John to go into the house with the child's parents. There was confusion with wailing and crying.

Jesus asked, "Don't cry; the child is not dead she is only sleeping".

They started making fun of Him and that is the reason why He kept all the others out. He went to the dead child, took her hand and said to her, "Talitha koum", which means in Aramaic, little girl, I tell you to get up!

She got up at once and started walking about. Then Jesus told them to get her something to eat. "The news about this spread all over that part of the country" *(Matthew 9:26).*

Jairus must have been a good Pharisee and deserved to have his daughter restored to life because of his faith in Jesus. The woman with the bleeding disorder, Tableda, must have prayed desperately to God too. Her faith made her well. If only we can have such faith in Jesus, the Physician, the Healer, we will have less stress in our lives.

TAMAR (Palm Tree)

Genesis 38:24

Quote: Her life is like that of a palm tree trying to survive in the strong winds; forces beyond her control.

Judah left his brothers after Joseph was sold to the Midianites. They in turn sold Joseph to Potiphar one of the officers of the pharaoh. Judah went to stay with a man named Hirah. There he met a lovely Canaanite lady and married her. She bore him a son named Er, then another two sons, Onan and Shelah.

His first son Er was evil and his conduct displeased the Lord. He married a young girl called Tamar. Er died soon after his marriage. Judah then told his second son Onan to sleep with his brother's widow, Tamar, so that she could have descendants. He did sleep with Tamar, but "he let the semen spill on the ground, so that there would be no children for his brother". He did not win favour with the Lord, so he too died.

Then Judah told his daughter-in-law to return to her father's house and remain there a widow till his son Shelah grew up. In fact he was afraid that this son too would be killed, so he told her to go. Tamar went to her father's house. Years later Judah's wife fell sick and died. Judah, now a widower, went to Timnah to see sheep being sheared. Shelah was now fully grown but his father did not give his son to Tamar.

Tamar was informed that her father-in-law was going to Timnah. She wanted to see him and maybe win his favour. When Judah saw her sitting by the roadside on the road to Timnah he got interested in her, and since she had covered her face (covered to disguise herself) he thought she was a prostitute.

He questioned her, "All right, how much do you charge?"

She asked cheekily, "What will you give me?"

He said, "I will send you a young goat from my flock". The flock was not there with him.

She replied, "All right, if you will give me something to keep as a pledge until you send the goat".

He asked: "What shall I give you as a pledge?"

Tamar replied, "Your seal with its cord and the stick you are carrying". He readily gave these to her. Then Judah had intercourse with Tamar and she became pregnant.

Judah called his friend Hirah to take the goat to the woman and get back what he pledged. Hirah searched for her all over in the region — no luck. "Where is the prostitute who was here by the road?"

The men he inquired of replied, "There never has been a prostitute here". Hirah returned to Judah and reported to him that there had not been a prostitute there for a long time.

So Judah felt bad and said that maybe she should keep the items, but at least he tried to search for her and pay her. He did not want to make a commotion or people would laugh at him going in search of a prostitute, so he did not pay for her services.

Anyway, after three months, someone told Judah that his daughter-in-law Tamar was pregnant. Judah was furious and this was too much for him to bear. So he ordered his men, "Take her out and burn her to death". She had brought shame to his name.

As she was being dragged to be burnt, she sent word to Judah, "I am pregnant by the man who owns these things". Then she showed the seal with its cord and the stick.

Judah instantly felt ashamed. He admitted he was the culprit. "I should have given her to my son Shelah in marriage".

Tamar gave birth to twins and named them Perez and Zerah. Perez, you might recall was the ancestor of a great person — who else? — King David! David, by the way, was the ancestor of Our Lord Jesus.

Think It Over:

Goodness always triumphs. Daily do good deeds and the graces increase in your favour. Did you do something good today?

TAMAR, DAUGHTER OF DAVID

(Palm Tree)
2 Samuel 13:1-21

Absalom was famous for his good looks. He had thick long hair and no physical defects. David also loved his son very much.

Amnon, another of David's sons, fell in love with Tamar, his step-sister. His love was so overwhelming "that he became ill, because it seemed impossible for him to have her". He confided these thoughts to Jonadab, who was the son of David's brother, Shammah. Jonadab was an evil man and gave bad advice to Amnon.

He asked Amnon to pretend that he was sick and go to bed. When his father went to visit him he should request him to send his sister Tamar to come and help feed him. So Amnon did the pretending and the king fell for it. David asked Tamar to go and feed the young man.

Tamar took some dough, prepared it and baked some cakes and brought them to him. Amnon told her, "Send everyone away". Then he asked her to give him the cakes. As she sat feeding him, he grabbed her and asked her to sleep with him.

"No," she said. "Don't force me to do such a degrading thing! That's awful!" In spite of all her protests he overpowered her and raped her.

Then, after this act, "Amnon was filled with a deep hatred for her". He told her, "Get out!"

"No," she answered. "To send me away like this is a greater crime than what you just did!"

But Amnon was furious and he called his personal servant and shouted "Get this woman out of my sight! Throw her out and lock the door!" The servant pulled her out and locked the door.

Tamar at that time was wearing the long robe of a princess with full sleeves. She was sorrowful. She sprinkled ashes on her head, tore her robe, and with her head buried in her hands she came out crying. When her brother Absalom saw her in this condition he asked her, "Has Amnon molested you . . . ? He is your half-brother, so don't tell anyone about it". She lived in Absalom's house sad and lonely. When King David heard about it he was very angry but did not do much to rectify the situation.

Two years after this incident, Absalom arranged for a special banquet and he invited all the sons of the king, including Amnon. At the function the servants got Amnon drunk and on instructions from Absalom killed him for the crime he had committed.

When King David heard that his son Amnon was murdered he mourned for him. The other brothers also left the company of Absalom. Absalom then fled and went to live with King Talmai of Geshur for three years. King David, after his mourning for Amnon, now yearned for his missing son Absalom. It was Joab who arranged for Absalom's return to his father. But this was a short-lived joy. A rebellion followed and Absalom was killed.

It may sound confusing but, as you will remember, Absalom too had one beautiful daughter named Tamar *(2 Samuel 14:27),* and you also read "David's son Absalom had a beautiful unmarried sister named Tamar" *(2 Samuel 13:1).* It was this sister who was raped not his daughter.

There are three Tamars in the Bible, one being the lady raped by Judah. Somehow it doesn't encourage one to give this name to any beautiful girl.

Think It Over:

In the world there are many forms of abuse in which women are involved. Much of this stems from discrimination and bias, from ignorance and tradition. Rape and domestic violence are on the increase even in the 21st Century. Help the victims.

THEBEZIRA (Woman of Thebez)

Judges 9:1-56

There was once a very bad man in Israel who killed many people. Interestingly, he had seventy brothers. This was because his father had a tremendous sexual appetite and had several wives. He was one of Israel's greatest warriors and his name was Gideon. Nobody really knows how many daughters he fathered.

One of his sons was Abimelech. This was the bad son. He went to his mother's hometown, Shechem, and asked them, "Do you want all those seventy sons of Gideon to reign over you? Would you not rather wish that it were I alone, who am your near relation?"

This incident is mentioned in the Book of Judges. This Book deals with events in a period which was known for lawlessness that followed after the death of Joshua.

The people of Shechem decided to follow Abimelech as their leader. They gave him money from the temple of Baal-of-the-Covenant, and with this money "he hired a bunch of worthless scoundrels to join him". He managed to kill all the sons of his famous warrior father, Gideon, except for the youngest who was named Jotham, because he went into hiding. Then Abimelech was crowned king. The seventy sons who were killed lived in Ophrah, the hometown of Gideon.

Jotham came out of his hiding and appealed to the people to reject the new king, his brother, but it was of no use. So, he ran away to another city called Beer.

Abimelech ruled Israel for three years. During this time he waged several wars against many Israelite chieftains. One of them was Gaal, son of Ebed. He fought with some of his own in a form of rebellion. There was chaos. He even razed Shechem to the ground and killed the inhabitants. Those who sought shelter in the temple and the fort, he piled wood around it and burnt the men and women inside to death.

"Then Abimelech went to Thebez, surrounded that city, and captured it". There was a strong tower there, and all the people barricaded themselves inside it to escape this savage king. When Abimelech came to attack the tower he went to the door to set fire to the tower. But luck was against him. A strong woman who was taking refuge in the tower carried a millstone up the tower and on to the roof. As Abimelech was trying to set fire to the tower she accurately dropped the millstone on his unsuspecting head causing it to fracture.

Abimelech was hurt very badly but managed to utter to his soldier friend, "Draw your sword and kill me. I don't want it said that a woman killed me".

So his friend stabbed him to save his honour and killed him. This act of the young woman of Thebez saved the city and the inhabitants. "Hurrah for Thebezira!"

Think It Over:

There are many roads to take when you find yourself at the crossroads. Take the right road with noble intentions. Sometimes the road less travelled is the better road. The road towards God is often a difficult road with thorny bushes. Seek divine assistance.

TRESUNA (Proverb-31 Woman)
Proverbs 31:10-31

The Book of Proverbs has thirty-one chapters. It is a compilation of religious and moral teachings in the form of aphorisms and proverbs for our daily life. The first chapter begins with the words: "The proverbs of Solomon, son of David and king of Israel. Here are proverbs that will help you to recognize wisdom and good advice . . . They can teach you how to live intelligently and how to be honest, just and fair".

Most of the advice comes with the introduction, "My child", do this and that. Then comes the final section, that is chapter 31, under the heading, "The Capable Wife".

> "How hard it is to find a capable wife!
> She is worth far more than jewels!
> Her husband put his confidence in her,
> And he will never be poor.
> As long as she lives, she does him good
> And never harm. . . .
> She knows the value of everything she makes,
> And works late into the night. . . .
> Give her credit for all she does.
> She deserves the respect of everyone".

Certainly it is in praise of the ideal woman.

Proverb 31 also forms a part of the advice to the king by King Lemuel's mother: "You are my own dear son, the answer to my prayers. What shall I tell you? Don't spend all your energy on sex and all your money on women; they have destroyed kings. Listen, Lemuel. Kings should not drink wine or have a craving for alcohol. When they drink, they forget the laws and ignore the rights of people in need. Alcohol is for people who are dying, for those who are in misery. Let them drink and forget their poverty and unhappiness".

The Book of Proverbs has also interesting and valuable advice on women (especially immoral women) and adultery. The aspect of a nagging wife is mentioned in three separate proverbs. For example, Proverb 27:15: "A nagging wife is like water going drip-drip-drip on a rainy day. How can you keep her quiet?"!

Who Is the Ideal Wife?

This is a difficult question to answer. There are cultural and tribal customs that have high demands and expectations for women.

In the Taliban era, women were expected as wives to submit completely to the husbands. They could view others only through the veil. They had no rights at all.

In the advanced countries where there are working mothers, women have to wear several feathers in their cap. They are the homemaker and have to please a lot of souls. The ideal wife is the one who takes the vocation with humility and dedication to her family.

It is interesting to note, in the genealogy of Jesus, that there are fourteen generations from Abraham to David. Also from David to the Babylonic captivity there are fourteen generations. There are also fourteen generations from the Babylonic captivity to the birth of Jesus.

TRYPAULA (Woman in Paul's Mind)
Ephesians 5:21

Sometime ago I was at UCLA (Los Angeles) and saw some demonstrators carrying placards and shouting some slogans along Westwood Boulevard. These were the gays, lesbians, HIV support groups and the AIDS sufferers or workers. What caught my attention was placards saying: "Down with Paul 5:21". "Down with Ephesians 5:33".

My companion was amused and asked me, "What has the great missionary St Paul got to do with these people?" Yes, why the hatred for Paul the Apostle of the Gentiles? He belonged to the 1st Century and we are now in the 21st Century.

Before you get me wrong, please take note of this fact: I have a great admiration for Paul and the good work that he did. I have also gone to the areas he travelled by boat to see first-hand the extent of his zeal to reach the multitudes and preach the message of Jesus Christ. I have also helped treat a few women who were faint of heart and collapsed, overcome by emotion, on beholding the site where he was martyred by the Romans. If it were not for Paul many of us would not have the Word of God or become Christians.

Paul was no woman-hater or one who belittled women. He has been terribly misunderstood by many single mothers and liberal-thinking women. The woman according to Paul's mind must be a gentle lady. Paul was helped by many women in his apostolic work. He has praised these women in his Epistles. Paul is aware of androgens. What gives man a bad name is his quick temper and strong voice. Androgens are the male hormones that make the male physically powerful. Paul wants women to allow men to be men. Women have their speciality that is distinct — the milk of human kindness that is more characteristic of females. A women should be humble, kind and loving.

Women in the 1st Century were confined to the homes and were not given any opportunities. Being physically weaker, they were advised to be subject to the physically stronger beings. On other matters women are stronger and are even more durable. Insurance statistics show that women outlive men. Nutritive surveys show that they can withstand hunger and starvation for a longer period than men. This is because they have more fat (adipose tissue) in their bodies that serves as stored calories. Men have more muscle bulk and less fatty tissue. Emotionally too women are stronger (their tears can move and soften even the most hard-hearted of men). Psychologically they can handle more stress because they use the two cerebral hemispheres of the brain to think. Men fly off their heads or hats with a quicker reaction-on-instinct basis, only to regret it later. Women think of the consequences and act with maternal considerations; their protective instincts make them better savers than men. If a man is rich it is because of the saving instincts of a woman!

By the way, if you want to sell some products (and that's what advertisement hype is all about), put a female on the billboards or posters. Women in the 21st Century are at the reins of major businesses and have come to show their worth, but conservative ideas still prevail. And, don't blame Paul.

Ephesians 5:33

" . . . . wives must submit themselves completely to their husbands".

VASHTI (Beautiful)
Esther 1:1-22

To understand this story we must consider the customs of Middle Eastern countries, like Persia, where women do not have any rights in society. This is true even today. They are forbidden to drive cars and pursue certain studies. There are restrictions in their daily lives too. The Islamic revolution of Ayatollah Khomeini was to usher in the old customs and traditions, where women were considered inferior creatures and where their "aurat" body shape should be hidden from the eyes of beholders and reserved only for the husbands.

Vashti (the name means beautiful) was the queen of King Xerxes. He was proud of her and her beauty and wanted to show her off to his officials and invitees. He threw a great banquet for this purpose, but the queen had her own ideas. She denied him his request, and instead had her own banquet for an all-women gathering. The king felt insulted, and what once was intense love, now was transformed into a burning rage of hatred for being scorned. He consulted his male officials who, of course, encouraged him to dishonour her by removing her from the position of queen. This was not the end of it; they also advised him to seek a new queen.

What was Vashti's great crime? In the eyes of the Western World, she did not commit any serious crime. She had her reasons. The king wanted to parade her like one of his beautiful possessions. She was to be an item for the drunken men during the seven-day banquet to view and declare, "Yes, she is truly beautiful, true to her name. Even the crown fits her appropriately".

Vashti was the progenitor of the Women's Liberation Front. Maybe she was against the exploitation of women and 'flesh parades'. There are organizations in a number of countries presently which abhor such pageants and parades. Anyway, Vashti must have been shocked that her decision to abstain from the banquet caused such a change of heart in the king.

This brings us to the issue of what we must consider as true beauty and virtue. Beauty must not be in the physical and in body-surface anatomy. It must be in the deep sentiments of a person's inner self. This is what Peter mentions in his Epistle *(1 Peter 3:3-4)*.

Beauty should not be from external ornaments of hairstyles and expensive jewellery, "Instead, your beauty should consist of your true inner self, the ageless beauty of a gentle and quiet spirit, which is of the greatest value in God's sight".

Peter also says ". . . husbands must live with your wives with the proper understanding that they are the weaker sex". Evidently, King Xeres and Vashti did not have much understanding and dialogue.

What was Vashti's fault? Was it such a great crime that she should have been punished with such disgrace?

Could she have prevented the course of events that led to her being 'expelled'?

If this had not happened, Esther would not have come on the scene and the course of history would have been different for the Hebrews. All this was in God's plan of salvation. This is a mystery and a lesson.

VERITAMA (True Mother)

1 Kings 3:16-19

Once upon a time, during the reign of King Solomon of Jerusalem, there were two mothers. The two women were involved in a bitter argument. The quarrel was a serious one and they fought. The matter was brought to the attention of the king.

The whole incident started this way, according to the women: it was a case of baby stealing. Let us bear in mind that this was in a century before the birth of Christ. There were no blood tests or DNA-matching technology.

"One day two prostitutes came and presented themselves before King Solomon. One of them said, "Your Majesty, this woman and I live in the same house, and I gave birth to a baby boy at home while she was there. Two days after my child was born she also gave birth to a baby boy" *(1 Kings 3:16-19)*.

It seems one night the other woman accidentally rolled over her baby and killed the baby, during her sleep. She discovered what she had done and so in the night she took the live baby and switched it with her dead child. Next morning the woman discovered to her horror, when she was going to nurse her baby, that the child next to her was dead and it was not her baby. Each of them knew well their own child. So the argument arose and King Solomon had this difficult task of finding out who was the true mother.

King Solomon said, "Each of you claims that the living child is hers . . . " So he called his soldier to bring a sword. "Cut the living child in two and give each woman half of it".

Now, the real mother was shocked by the decision and appealed to the king, "Please, Your Majesty, don't kill the child! Give it to her!"

But the other woman said, "Don't give it to either of us; go ahead and cut it in two".

King Solomon heard these words and knew by these utterances the truth of the matter. "Give it to the first woman — she is its real mother".

The people of Israel heard this and had great respect for King Solomon's wisdom. However, in the latter days of his rule he misused his wisdom to acquire more wives and concubines. In 1 Kings 11, we learn that, "Solomon married seven hundred princesses and also had three hundred concubines. They made him turn away from God [to worship foreign gods]".

Think It Over:

Nobody must say that we are born without talents. Count your blessings. You must appreciate the fact that you have several talents.

It is imperative that you recognize your assets — your talents. It is also very important that you develop your talents to glorify Almighty God!

Solomon received several talents but in the end he misused these for his own glory.

Go and watch the ants, says the writer of the Proverbs. She works hard all day. That's what you should do, otherwise you'll end up poor and be despised by people . . .

Such are the practical words of advice in the Bible. In fact the whole Bible encourages people to be active and not be lazy.

ZAREMA (The Widow of Zarephath)

1 Kings 17:8-24

Once there was a terrible drought in Israel. A prophet named Elijah from Tishbe in Gilead informed King Ahab that there would be no dew or rain for the next two or three years.

The Lord said to Elijah, "Leave this place and go east and hide yourself near the brook of Cherith, east of the Jordan. The brook will supply you with water to drink, and I have commanded ravens to bring you food there".

Elijah did as he was commanded. The ravens brought him bread in the morning and in the evening. He drank the water from the brook. After some time the brook dried up. Elijah was worried. The Lord spoke to him and asked him to go to the town of Zarephath, near Sidon, and stay there. "I have commanded a widow who lives there to feed you". What a strange announcement! The prophet packed up and left as he was asked.

As soon as he came to the town gate he saw the poor widow gathering firewood. He was very thirsty and he asked her, "Please bring me a drink of water". And as she left to fetch him a drink he shouted out, "And please bring me some bread, too".

The poor widow was shocked at the stranger making these requests. Soon she answered, "By the living Lord your God I swear that I haven't got any bread. All I have is a handful of flour in a bowl and a drop of olive-oil in a jar". She said she really came there to gather firewood to light a fire and bake the bread for the last meal for her and her son, "and then we will starve to death".

Elijah reassured her, "Don't worry. Go ahead and prepare your meal. But first make a small loaf from what you have and bring it to me, and then prepare the rest for you and your son". He told her the Lord had told him, "The bowl will not run out of flour or the jar run out of oil before that day that I, the Lord, send rain".

The widow could have refused to feed the stranger but she did as he asked. The miracle happened. The bowl did not run out of flour or the jar run out of oil. There was food in plenty for a long time.

Some time later, while Elijah was staying there, her son fell ill and died. The widow was upset and spoke thus, "Man of God, why did you do this to me? Did you come here to remind God of my sins and so cause my son's death?"

Elijah took the dead boy and carried him up to the room in the roof where he was staying. There he pleaded with God loudly, "O Lord my God, why have you done such a terrible thing to this widow? She has been kind enough to take care of me, and now you kill her son! O Lord my God, restore this child to life! The Lord answered his prayer. Elijah took the boy downstairs and handed him over to the jubilant mother. "Look, your son is alive!"

After this, on the third year of the famine, Elijah left on the instructions of the Lord to see King Ahab. Elijah knew this new command would be risky as Jezebel was out looking for him and other prophets to put them to death. Yet he left on his mission.

Think It Over:

In Judges 19:1-26 we read of a sad happening involving an unnamed woman (a concubine) and the Levite of Ephraim. She was raped and killed by sex perverts. She was from Bethlehem. The Levite cut the woman's body into twelve pieces and gave one to each tribe of Israel in disgust.

This started a civil war, the war against the Benjaminites. The Israelites won. Most of the fighting took place in the battlefield at Gibeah.

ZEBEDA (Zebedee's Wife)
Matthew 20:20-25; Mark 10:35-45

"Then the wife of Zebedee came to Jesus with her two sons, bowed before Him and asked Him a favour".

"What do you want?" Jesus asked her.

"Promise me that these two sons of mine will sit at your right and your left when you are king".

The sons of Zebedee were James and John. They were closely related to Him. In fact they were His first cousins. This is a strange request from a mother who must have had a tough time controlling the enthusiasm and spirit of her two sons. They were also referred to as the "sons of thunder".

The mother here is shown as a completely ignorant woman who does not know the mission of Jesus. She is only thinking of material gains. She wants her sons to become famous — not just blind followers of a man who talks and preaches about a kingdom. She is sure that Jesus will become a king because of growing popularity and performing miracles. She wants good position for her children. Nobody, even a well-intentioned mother, wants her children to follow a leader she is disillusioned with.

Now comes the interesting part. The other ten apostles did not like the interference of the mother. She came to use her influence on Jesus? She came to plead her sons' cause? Could the other apostles bring their mothers and Peter his mother-in-law too to ask for higher rankings?

Jesus called them all together and gave them a pep talk, as there was anger among the others. It was a conference to get back to the basics. He told them that service was the key note. The Son of Man "did not come to be served, but to serve and to give His life to redeem many people", Jesus instructed.

ZERUIAH

2 Samuel 16:9

When King David arrived at Bahurim, one of Saul's relatives, Shimei, came to meet him. He cursed him as soon as he saw him. He even threw stones at David and his officials.

"Murderer! Criminal! You took Saul's kingdom . . . you are ruined, you murderer!" He shouted profanities.

Abishai, whose mother was Zeruiah, said to King David, "Your Majesty, why do you let this dog curse you? Let me go over there and cut off his head!"

King David said, "This is none of your business. . . . My own son is trying to kill me; so why should you be surprised at this Benjaminite . . . ? Perhaps, the Lord will notice my misery and give me some blessings to take the place of his curse". David moved on and did not do anything.

Zeruiah had three sons, Joab, Abishai and Asahel. Abner was the commander of Saul's army. He fought and killed Asahel. The remaining brothers killed Abner in revenge. King David ordered the brothers to wear sackcloth and mourn for Abner. King David said, "These son's of Zeruiah are too violent for me".

Interestingly, King David, who did not approve of the actions of the sons of Zeruiah, later used Joab to have Uriah the Hittite killed. He gave the instructions in a letter. Joab did the job right and so David was able to acquire Uriah's wife. Joab was King David's confidant and commandant. He was the one who tried to bring peace between the king and his son, Absalom.

ZIONIMA (Daughter of Zion)
2 Kings 5:1-26

Even young girls have done their share to evangelize and spread the message of God's healing power. This aspect is shown in the story of a pretty young girl who was kidnapped by Naaman and his raiding party and taken away into slavery in Syria.

While in a foreign land and working as a slave for people who did not know the true God, she decided to show her Jewish heritage and faith in the true God. She noticed that Naaman had a terrible disease called leprosy, which at that time was considered incurable. The only one who could cure him of this was the true God of Israel.

So she narrated this to her mistress and convinced her: "I wish that my Master could go to the prophet who lives in Samaria! He would cure him of his disease".

Later on in the life of Our Lord we hear Him speak about this incident to the Jews in the synagogue at Nazareth. They got so incensed and angry that they took Him to the edge of the mountain cliff to push Him down, but He passed away in their midst. The timing was not ripe for Our Lord to die and neither too in that manner of death.

In this story of Naaman, the girl's faith was conveyed to the King of Syria. He had a great respect for Naaman so he went out of his way to write a letter to the King of Israel and offered the following gifts: Six thousand pieces of gold and thirty thousand pieces of silver and ten changes of fine clothes.

The Israeli king received the letter of introduction and it was the request for the cure. He was awfully angry and tore his garments (not because new fine clothes had arrived). Why? Because he felt it was impossible to cure the disease.

"How can the King of Syria expect me to cure this man? Does he think that I am God, with the power of life and death? It's plain that he is trying to start a quarrel with me!"

Elisha heard about this and volunteered to help. So Naaman went to see him. But Elisha did not go out to meet him. He sent his servant with the message that Naaman immerse himself in the River Jordan seven times.

Naaman was upset. What a simple request. He was familiar with the great rivers of Syria, Abana and Pharpar and did not think much about the tiny River Jordan.

Two issues upset Naaman: Firstly, the prophet Elisha, he felt, should have come to see him. Secondly, he expected the prophet to come and perform some hocus-pocus — he could have waved his hand over the diseased spots. But nothing dramatic happened.

This brings us to the subject of mediums and others who ask for favours and put up a lot of show. God does not want that. He wants repentance, obedience and humility. Our God is an all-merciful and forgiving God.

Naaman was upset but his aides counselled him to obey the holy prophet. Naaman did as he was advised and was surprised to see that he was cured. Naaman shouted out praises to the Lord. "Now I know that there is no god but the God of Israel . . . "

All this happened because of the faith and initiative of a young Israeli slave girl. The lesson to be learned from this: never give up speaking of God and His amazing saving grace.

ZIPPORAH (Hebrew: Sparrow)
Exodus 2:21

Zipporah was the daughter of a Midianite priest named Jethro, who had seven daughters and no son. One day when she and her sisters were tending sheep, a group of men came to disturb them. Moses at that time was a fugitive, who had escaped to the land of Midian. He was sitting by a well and the girls were there to fetch water from the well. Moses came to their rescue and later watered the animals for the girls.

When they returned home early that day their father enquired what had happened and the girls gave their story of how they were rescued by the Egyptian.

"Why did you leave the man out there? Go and invite him to eat with us". Moses after this came to live with this family and married Zipporah, the eldest daughter.

Moses had two sons through her, the eldest he named Gershom (meaning foreigner, because he, Moses, considered himself a foreigner in Midian).

Moses left for Egypt to do the will of God, who appeared in the burning bush. He took his wife and his sons and the special stick to go to Egypt because he considered it safe: "those who wanted to kill you are dead" *(Exodus 4:19)*.

It must have been a tough time to be Moses' wife, for Zipporah. Firstly, she was a foreigner. Secondly, she had lived a very simple life with her father and her sisters looking after the sheep in Midian. Now, she has become an important man's wife. Moses, the leader of the Jews, and of the Exodus into Sinai and the Promised Land.

There were too many events and the drama of human life was exceedingly full of emotion. There were times when the people did not listen to Moses. They complained about him and even plotted against his ways.

Moses must have been very difficult at times. Firstly, he had problems arguing with God about the difficult job of leading the Israelites out of Egypt. Secondly he had the difficult job of arguing with the stubborn pharaoh. "Let my people go," Moses pleaded. But it was not easy for the pharaoh to do so.

Zipporah had other problems too. Miriam and Aaron did not approve of her as she was a foreigner.

In Numbers 12:1-16 we learn that Moses married a Cushite woman, and Miriam and Aaron criticized him for it. Cushites were regarded as Midiantes or Ethiopians. The Book of Numbers mentions that the Lord was angry with Miriam and called all three — Moses, Aaron and Miriam — to the tent to stand in His presence. He caused a skin disease to come about on Miriam but Moses pleaded for it to be healed. The Lord nevertheless let her be isolated for seven days in solitary confinement and she was forgiven.

The words of the Lord were harsh. "I have put him in charge of all my people Israel. So I speak to him face to face, clearly and not in riddles; he has even seen my form! How dare you speak against my servant Moses?"

There is a difficult passage in the Bible that is unclear and perhaps translated so. It deals with Zipporah taking a sharp stone to cut her son's foreskin and touching the feet of Moses with it. It is said that God was displeased with Moses and wanted to kill him, so Zipporah did this act to win God's favour *(Exodus 4:25-26)*.

Her words were, "Because of the rite of circumcision she said to Moses, 'You are a husband of blood to me'. And so the Lord spared Moses's life." Probably, this passage exists to show how Zipporah, a foreigner and one who was despised, was wanting to be accepted as saving the life of Moses.

Anyway, ironically, Moses sent Zipporah and the sons back to Jethro in Midian after this act by Zipporah. They were to meet again in a desert rendezvous in the Sinai after the Exodus. Jethro brought about the family reunion. What a place for a family reunion.

ZOAN (Aramaic: To Borrow)
2 Kings 4:1-8

The widow of a member of the group of prophets went to Elisha and said, "Sir, my husband has died! As you know, he was a God-fearing man . . . " There was a big problem.

Her husband had borrowed a certain sum of money from a loan shark who was now threatening to take her two sons as slaves in lieu of the debt. There was no way out, as they were very poor.

Elisha asked her if they had any assets at home which she could sell. The widow replied that all she had was "a small jar of olive-oil". The husband had been a very honest and upright man who had not cheated anybody, and so now the widow and her two sons were at the mercy of this man who had loaned the money.

This brings out the fact that every family should set aside some savings for a rainy day. I am advocating people taking out insurance policies and putting aside some savings for future use. In this case the widow and her family had nothing and so had no means to repay their loan except by seeking divine assistance.

This happened at a very difficult time in the history of Israel. This incident is in the second Book of Kings where we read of disasters, namely the fall of the Kingdom of Judah, the fall of the Kingdom of Israel, the destruction of Jerusalem by King Nebuchadnezzar in 587 BC and the fall of Samaria and the end of the Northern Kingdom in 722 BC. Also we read about Elisha, the prophet who succeeded Elijah. The disasters took place because the kings and the people sinned against the Lord with different forms of worship of foreign gods and goddesses.

But, Elisha managed to help the poor widow and her two young sons. How? He had no money but he could work miracles. He was a man of God. Priests are a class of people between the faithful and the Kingdom of God. Prophets were mediators between God and the priests.

Elisha happened to know the widow because she was the wife of a member of a group of Prophets. "Go to your neighbours and borrow as many empty jars as you can", Elisha ordered. Zoan and her two boys had an easy order to follow: collect empty jars (and at that time there were many of these). It all depended on their initiative. People wanted to help the poor widow. Obviously, all the neighbourhood knew of their plight. The boys knew their fate. This was the last chance — to do something or to be carried away as slaves.

Elisha gave specific instructions. They were told to stay at home and lock the door. The widow had to pour a few drops of olive-oil into each of the jars from her small jar of oil.

Soon Zoan (the widow) and her two sons were busy. They realized that the empty jars were now filled to capacity. Elisha instructed, "Set each one aside as soon as it is full".

When she had filled all the jars, she asked if there were any more. She was tired. "That was the last one", one of her sons answered. The olive-oil stopped flowing out. Elisha told Zoan to sell the olive-oil and pay off her debts and she could then live comfortably from the olive-oil sales. She became the local olive-oil merchant.

The Moral:

Turn to God for help.

Only God can help you.

God will send His ministers to work miracles for you.

Additional List of Popular Biblical Names of Women

Abbey — Hebrew — father's joy. From Abigail. Variations — Abigail, Abbe, Abbi, Abby, Abbye, Abe, Gael, Gail, Gale, Gayel, Gayle.

Abra — Hebrew — mother of many. She was one of the wives of Solomon.

Adah — Hebrew — ornament. She was one of Lamech's two wives (*Genesis 4:19*), the other wife was Zillah.

Adina — Hebrew — voluptuous. Variations — Adena, Dina.

Amariah — Hebrew — God has spoken. Old Testament name popular with Puritans.

Anita — Hebrew — graceful. Variation — Nita.

Ann, Anne — Hebrew — graceful. Originally Hannah. Variations — Ana, Anette, Anja, Annette, Nancy, Nan, Nita; Sheena (Scottish).

Annamaria — Hebrew — graceful, bitter. A combination of Anne and Mary. Variations — Anne Marie, Anna Marie.

Aurea — Hebrew — daughter of Jehovah. Variation — Aurelia.

Bathsheba — Hebrew — daughter of an oath. Variation — Sheba.

Becky — Hebrew — knotted cord or faithful wife. Shortened form of Rebecca.

Bernice — Roman — bold. Variation — Berna.

Bess — Hebrew — God satisfies. Variations — Bessie, Bessy, Betsy.

Bethany — Aramaic — house of poverty. Variations — Betha, Betty, Bettrys (Welsh Beatrice).

Beulah — Hebrew — matronly, married. Variation — Beula.

Carmel — Hebrew — garden. Variations — Carmela, Carmelina, Carmelita, Carmen, Carmencita, Carmita, Lita.

Damaris — Greek — calf, gentle.

Danielle — Hebrew — God has judged. Variations — Dannie, Danelle, Danella.

Debbie — Hebrew — bee. Original form Deborah. Variations — Debby, Debbi, Deb, Debora, Debra (also Melissa in Greek).

Delilah — Hebrew — delight.

Dinah — Hebrew — avenged, lawsuit. Her brothers avenged her.

Drusilla — Hebrew — learned. Jewish wife of Roman Governor Festus.

Eden — Hebrew — delight.

Elizabeth — Hebrew — God is my satisfaction. Variations — Elise, Eliza, Elisabeth.

Esther — Hebrew — star. Persian — myrtle. Originally Hadassah in Hebrew meaning myrtle. The myrtle has star-like flowers.

Eve — Hebrew — life-giving. Name of the first woman, given by Adam. Variations — Eva, Evie, Evita.

Hamutal — Mother of King Zedekiah of Jerusalem and daughter of Jeremiah. She was taken prisoner to Babylon.

Hannah — Hebrew — grace. Mother of Samuel. Variations — Hana, Hanna, Anna.

Hoglah — Sister of Thizra.

Huldah — Hebrew — mole, a prophetess. Variation — Huldah.

Jael — Hebrew — wild goat. The slayer of Sisera the Canaanite general.

Jemima — Hebrew — dove. One of the three daughters of Job. Variations — Jem, Jamima, Jemie, Gemmy, Jemmie, Jemmy.

Jessie — Hebrew — Jehovah has favoured. Feminine form of Jesse, father of David. Variations — Jess, Jessy.

Joan — Hebrew — Jehovah has favoured. Feminine form of John. Variations — Gianna, Giannina, Giovanna, Jan, Janette, Jaris, Jeanne, Jenni, Jess.

Jodie — Hebrew — Jewish woman, from Judah. Variations — Jodie, Jody.

Jordan — Hebrew — flowing down. Variations — Jordane, Gordana.

Josephine — Hebrew — may Jehovah be praised. Feminine form of Joseph.

Judith — Hebrew — Jewish woman, from Judah.

Judy — Hebrew — Jewish woman.

Julia — Hebrew — chaste. Variations — Juliana, Julie.

Keren — Hebrew — horn of stibium (this is a cosmetic for the eye). One of Job's three daughters.

Kerenhappuch — The full name of the above.

Keturah — Hebrew — fragrance. Abraham's second wife.

Kezia — Hebrew — Cassia, a condiment like cinnamon. One of Job's daughters.

Leah — Hebrew — heifer. The first wife of Jacob. Variation — Lee.

Libby — Hebrew — God is my satisfaction. Variation — Elizabeth, Lib, Libbie.

Lily — Hebrew — God is my satisfaction. Variation — Elizabeth, Lilly.

Maachah — Queen mother, arrand mother of the good King Asa of Israel.

Magdalena — Hebrew — woman of Magdala. The name of Mary of Magdala (Tower). She could be the sister of Martha and Lazarus. Variations — Madelene, Made, Lena.

Mahalath — Ishmael's daughter. She married Esau.

Mahlah — Daughter of Zelophehad (see Thizra).

Marlene — Hebrew — a combination of Maria and Lena (from Magdalene).

Martha — Aramaic — the feminine form for man in Aramaic, Literally lady. She is believed to be the sister of Mary Magdalene and Lazarus. Variations — Marty, Marita.

Mary — Hebrew — bitter. The name in Hebrew is spelt only with consonants MRYM. The Latin form is Maria and it sounds melodious. Variations — Welsh: Mair. Scottish: Moira. German: Mame. French: Mara, Maria. Spanish/Italian: Mariam, Mariamme, Mariana, Marianna, Marianne, Marie, Mariel, Marietta, Marilyn, Marion, Mariquita, Marisa, Mariska, Mina, Mareta, Maryse. Russian: Marsha, Masha. Irish: Maire, Maureen, Mitzi, Mollie, Molly, May. Combinations — MaryAnne, Mary Lou, Marie-Claude.

Michelle — Hebrew — who is like God. Feminine form of Michael. Variations — Michal, Michel, Micky, Michelle.

Milcah — Nahor's wife. Nahor was brother of Abraham. Her father was Haran.

Naamah — King Rheboam's mother, an Ammonitess. Sister of Tubal Cain and daughter of Zillah.

Nancy — Hebrew — graceful. Derived from Hannah and also Ann.

Noah — Sister of Thirza.

Phebe — Greek — shining one. Also spelt Phoebe (*Romans 16:1*).

Priscilla — Roman family name — little Prisca is the literal form. It occurs in Paul's letter to Timothy. Variations — Cilla, Prissy.

Rachel — Hebrew — ewe. She was the daughter of Laban and the wife of Jacob. Variations — Rae, Ray, Shelly, Raquel, Rachael.

Rebecca — Hebrew — faithful. Wife of Isaac and mother of Jacob and Esau. Variations — Becca, Becky, Rebeca, Rebeka, Rivkah (Hebrew).

Rhoda — Greek — from Rhodes, the island of roses. She is mentioned in Acts 12. Variations — Rhoda, Rose.

Rizpah — Hebrew — hot coal. King Saul's concubine who bore him two sons.

Ruth — Hebrew — a vision of beauty. She was a Moabite, daughter-in-law of Naomi.

Salome — Aramaic — peace. It is the Greek form of the Hebrew Shalom.

Sapphira — Greek — sapphire. It is a Biblical name. Her husband was Ananias. Variations — Sapphira, Sephira.

Sarah — Hebrew — princess. Abraham's wife.

Sharon — Hebrew — princess. Rose of Sharon appears in the Song of Solomon.

Susanna — Hebrew — Lily. Variations — Susie, Susan.

Tabitha — Aramaic — antelope, gazelle. The Greek name is Dorcas. (She is mentioned in Acts 9.) Variation — Taby.

Tamara — Hebrew — palm tree. Variations — Tamis, Tammy.

Thekla — Greek — divine fame. She was a saint — St Thekla of Iconium. According to the Acts of St Paul she was a convert of St Paul.

Tirzah — Hebrew — acceptance. She was one of the daughters of Zelophehad in the Book of Numbers — Chapter 26. The other daughters were Mahlah, Noah, Hoglah and Milcah. They had no brothers and so after their father died they approached Moses about their inheritance. So because of this problem Moses received from God new instructions and made new rules about property inheritance — that daughters should be next in line of inheritance after the sons, or in the absence of sons.

Tryphena — Greek — delicate. Tryphena and Tryphose are two names in St Paul's Letters to the Romans. Variation — Triffy.

Veronica — Latin — true image. According to strong Christian tradition there was a woman who wiped the face of Jesus Christ as He walked carrying His cross to Calvary. She used her veil and the impression of His face came to be imprinted on the cloth. She is the patron saint of photographers. Variations — Vera, Verona, Verena, Voni, Ronnie.

Vashti — Persian — beautiful. Wife of King Xerxes.

Zarema — The widow of Zarephath.

Zillah — Hebrew — shade. She is mentioned in Genesis 4 as one of the two wives of Lamech. The other wife was Adah.

Zipporah — Hebrew — sparrow. The daughter of Jethro, the high priest of Midian. She was the wife of Moses. Variations — Zippora, Zip, Zipparo.

The Bad Women

Of all the women in the Bible only a few stand out as bad. These can be looked upon as a handful that worked against the plan of God's salvation.

Jezebel — daughter of King Ethbaal and wife of King Ahab.

Queen Athaliah — King Ahab's daughter.

Salome — the dancer who had John the Baptist beheaded.

Herodias — the adulterous wife of Philip, who was the brother of King Herod.

Delilah — who brought down the great Samson.

Potipharina — the rich woman who accused Joseph unjustly of attempted rape.

Fiera — the girl who accused Peter of being one of the Apostles and wanted him arrested and punished.

Gomer — the adulterous wife of Hosea, the prophet.

Maachah — the influential mother of King Asa. She was bad. She put up obscene images of the pagan goddess Asherah all over the Kingdom.

Nodiah — the false prophetess, nemesis of Nehemiah.

Drusilla — the Jewess wife of the governor Felix. The governor was a corrupt man "Who was hoping Paul would give him some money".

Zeresh — the wife of Haman the Agagite who proposed the gallows for Mordecai.

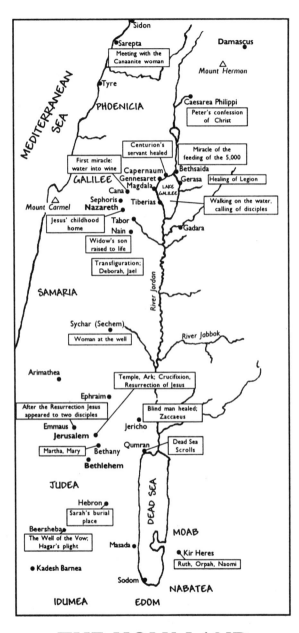

THE HOLY LAND